Developing
Essential Understanding
of
Geometry
for Teaching Mathematics *in*
Grades 9–12

D1205523

Nathalie Sinclair
Simon Fraser University
Burnaby, British Columbia

David Pimm
University of Alberta
Edmonton, Alberta

Melanie Skelin
Surrey Schools
Surrey, British Columbia

Rose Mary Zbiek
Series Editor
The Pennsylvania State University
University Park, Pennsylvania

NATIONAL COUNCIL OF
TEACHERS OF MATHEMATICS

Copyright © 2012 by
The National Council of Teachers of Mathematics, Inc.
1906 Association Drive, Reston, VA 20191-1502
(703) 620-9840; (800) 235-7566; www.nctm.org
All rights reserved
Second printing 2013

Library of Congress Cataloging-in-Publication Data

Developing essential understanding of geometry for teaching
mathematics in grades 9-12 / Nathalie Sinclair, David Pimm, Melanie
Skelin.
      p. cm.
   Includes bibliographical references.
   ISBN 978-0-87353-692-9
   1. Geometry--Study and teaching (Secondary) 2. Education, Secondary.
I. Pimm, David. II. Skelin, Melanie. III. Title.
   QA461.S5585 2012
   516.0071'2--dc23
                        2011053458

The National Council of Teachers of Mathematics is the public voice of mathematics education, supporting teachers to ensure equitable mathematics learning of the highest quality for all students through vision, leadership, professional development, and research.

Printed in the United States of America

Contents

Foreword

Teaching mathematics in prekindergarten–grade 12 requires a special understanding of mathematics. Effective teachers of mathematics think about and beyond the content that they teach, seeking explanations and making connections to other topics, both inside and outside mathematics. Students meet curriculum and achievement expectations when they work with teachers who know what mathematics is important for each topic that they teach.

The National Council of Teachers of Mathematics (NCTM) presents the Essential Understanding Series in tandem with a call to focus the school mathematics curriculum in the spirit of *Curriculum Focal Points for Prekindergarten through Grade 8 Mathematics: A Quest for Coherence*, published in 2006, and *Focus in High School Mathematics: Reasoning and Sense Making*, released in 2009. The Essential Understanding books are a resource for individual teachers and groups of colleagues interested in engaging in mathematical thinking to enrich and extend their own knowledge of particular mathematics topics in ways that benefit their work with students. The topic of each book is an area of mathematics that is difficult for students to learn, challenging to teach, and critical for students' success as learners and in their future lives and careers.

Drawing on their experiences as teachers, researchers, and mathematicians, the authors have identified the big ideas that are at the heart of each book's topic. A set of essential understandings—mathematical points that capture the essence of the topic—fleshes out each big idea. Taken collectively, the big ideas and essential understandings give a view of a mathematics that is focused, connected, and useful to teachers. Links to topics that students encounter earlier and later in school mathematics and to instruction and assessment practices illustrate the relevance and importance of a teacher's essential understanding of mathematics.

On behalf of the Board of Directors, I offer sincere thanks and appreciation to everyone who has helped to make this series possible. I extend special thanks to Rose Mary Zbiek for her leadership as series editor. I join the Essential Understanding project team in welcoming you to these books and in wishing you many years of continued enjoyment of learning and teaching mathematics.

Henry Kepner
President, 2008–2010
National Council of Teachers of Mathematics

Preface

From prekindergarten through grade 12, the school mathematics curriculum includes important topics that are pivotal in students' development. Students who understand these ideas cross smoothly into new mathematical terrain and continue moving forward with assurance.

However, many of these topics have traditionally been challenging to teach as well as learn, and they often prove to be barriers rather than gateways to students' progress. Students who fail to get a solid grounding in them frequently lose momentum and struggle in subsequent work in mathematics and related disciplines.

The Essential Understanding Series identifies such topics at all levels. Teachers who engage students in these topics play critical roles in students' mathematical achievement. Each volume in the series invites teachers who aim to be not just proficient but outstanding in the classroom—teachers like you—to enrich their understanding of one or more of these topics to ensure students' continued development in mathematics.

How much do you need to know?

To teach these challenging topics effectively, you must draw on a mathematical understanding that is both broad and deep. The challenge is to know considerably more about the topic than you expect your students to know and learn.

Why does your knowledge need to be so extensive? Why must it go above and beyond what you need to teach and your students need to learn? The answer to this question has many parts.

To plan successful learning experiences, you need to understand different models and representations and, in some cases, emerging technologies as you evaluate curriculum materials and create lessons. As you choose and implement learning tasks, you need to know what to emphasize and why those ideas are mathematically important.

While engaging your students in lessons, you must anticipate their perplexities, help them avoid known pitfalls, and recognize and dispel misconceptions. You need to capitalize on unexpected classroom opportunities to make connections among mathematical ideas. If assessment shows that students have not understood the material adequately, you need to know how to address weaknesses that you have identified in their understanding. Your understanding must be sufficiently versatile to allow you to represent the mathematics in different ways to students who don't understand it the first time.

In addition, you need to know where the topic fits in the full span of the mathematics curriculum. You must understand where your students are coming from in their thinking and where they are heading mathematically in the months and years to come.

Accomplishing these tasks in mathematically sound ways is a tall order. A rich understanding of the mathematics supports the varied work of teaching as you guide your students and keep their learning on track.

How can the Essential Understanding Series help?

The Essential Understanding books offer you an opportunity to delve into the mathematics that you teach and reinforce your content knowledge. They do not include materials for you to use directly with your students, nor do they discuss classroom management, teaching styles, or assessment techniques. Instead, these books focus squarely on issues of mathematical content—the ideas and understanding that you must bring to your preparation, in-class instruction, one-on-one interactions with students, and assessment.

How do the authors approach the topics?

For each topic, the authors identify "big ideas" and "essential understandings." The big ideas are mathematical statements of overarching concepts that are central to a mathematical topic and link numerous smaller mathematical ideas into coherent wholes. The books call the smaller, more concrete ideas that are associated with each big idea *essential understandings*. They capture aspects of the corresponding big idea and provide evidence of its richness.

The big ideas have tremendous value in mathematics. You can gain an appreciation of the power and worth of these densely packed statements through persistent work with the interrelated essential understandings. Grasping these multiple smaller concepts and through them gaining access to the big ideas can greatly increase your intellectual assets and classroom possibilities.

In your work with mathematical ideas in your role as a teacher, you have probably observed that the essential understandings are often at the heart of the understanding that you need for presenting one of these challenging topics to students. Knowing these ideas very well is critical because they are the mathematical pieces that connect to form each big idea.

How are the books organized?

Every book in the Essential Understanding Series has the same structure:

- The introduction gives an overview, explaining the reasons for the selection of the particular topic and highlighting some of the differences between what teachers and students need to know about it.

Big ideas and essential understandings are identified by icons in the books.

marks a big idea, and

marks an essential understanding.

- Chapter 1 is the heart of the book, identifying and examining the big ideas and related essential understandings.

- Chapter 2 reconsiders the ideas discussed in chapter 1 in light of their connections with mathematical ideas within the grade band and with other mathematics that the students have encountered earlier or will encounter later in their study of mathematics.

- Chapter 3 wraps up the discussion by considering the challenges that students often face in grasping the necessary concepts related to the topic under discussion. It analyzes the development of their thinking and offers guidance for presenting ideas to them and assessing their understanding.

The discussion of big ideas and essential understandings in chapter 1 is interspersed with questions labeled "Reflect." It is important to pause in your reading to think about these on your own or discuss them with your colleagues. By engaging with the material in this way, you can make the experience of reading the book participatory, interactive, and dynamic.

Reflect questions can also serve as topics of conversation among local groups of teachers or teachers connected electronically in school districts or even between states. Thus, the Reflect items can extend the possibilities for using the books as tools for formal or informal experiences for in-service and preservice teachers, individually or in groups, in or beyond college or university classes.

A new perspective

The Essential Understanding Series thus is intended to support you in gaining a deep and broad understanding of mathematics that can benefit your students in many ways. Considering connections between the mathematics under discussion and other mathematics that students encounter earlier and later in the curriculum gives the books unusual depth as well as insight into vertical articulation in school mathematics.

The series appears against the backdrop of *Principles and Standards for School Mathematics* (NCTM 2000), *Curriculum Focal Points for Prekindergarten through Grade 8 Mathematics: A Quest for Coherence* (NCTM 2006), *Focus in High School Mathematics: Reasoning and Sense Making* (NCTM 2009), and the Navigations Series (NCTM 2001–2009). The new books play an important role, supporting the work of these publications by offering content-based professional development.

The other publications, in turn, can flesh out and enrich the new books. After reading this book, for example, you might select hands-on, Standards-based activities from the Navigations books for your students to use to gain insights into the topics that the Essential Understanding books discuss. If you are teaching students in prekindergarten through grade 8, you might apply your deeper understanding as you present material related to the three focal points that *Curriculum Focal Points* identifies for instruction at your students' level. Or if you are teaching students in grades 9–12, you might use your understanding to enrich the ways in which you can engage students in mathematical reasoning and sense making as presented in *Focus in High School Mathematics.*

An enriched understanding can give you a fresh perspective and infuse new energy into your teaching. We hope that the understanding that you acquire from reading the book will support your efforts as you help your students grasp the ideas that will ensure their mathematical success.

The authors wish to thank their reviewers—David W. Henderson, Karen F. Hollebrands, Keith Jones, and Alfred S. Posamentier—for their insightful contributions to this volume.

Introduction

This book focuses on ideas about geometry. These are ideas that you need to understand thoroughly and be able to use flexibly to be highly effective in your teaching of mathematics in grades 9–12. The book discusses many mathematical ideas that are common in high school curricula, and it assumes that you have had a variety of mathematics experiences that have motivated you to delve into— and move beyond—the mathematics that you expect your students to learn.

The book is designed to engage you with these ideas, helping you to develop an understanding that will guide you in planning and implementing lessons and assessing your students' learning in ways that reflect the full complexity of geometry. A deep, rich understanding of ideas about geometry will enable you to communicate their influence and scope to your students, showing them how these ideas permeate the mathematics that they have encountered— and will continue to encounter—throughout their school mathematics experiences.

The understanding of geometry that you gain from this focused study thus supports the vision of *Principles and Standards for School Mathematics* (NCTM 2000): "Imagine a classroom, a school, or a school district where all students have access to high-quality, engaging mathematics instruction" (p. 3). This vision depends on classroom teachers who "are continually growing as professionals" (p. 3) and routinely engage their students in meaningful experiences that help them learn mathematics with understanding.

Why Geometry?

Like the topics of all the volumes in NCTM's Essential Understanding Series, geometry composes a major area of school mathematics that is crucial for students to learn but challenging for teachers to teach. Students in grades 9–12 need to understand geometric ideas well if they are to succeed in these grades and in their subsequent mathematics experiences. Learners often struggle with ideas about geometry. What does it mean to say that a reflection is a transformation—a function—or why does it matter that we state definitions carefully when we all know what particular geometric figures look like? The importance of properties of geometric objects and the many ways in which properties are embedded in diagrams and definitions make it essential for teachers of grades 9–12 to understand geometry extremely well themselves. In addition, ideas of geometry are used across the whole of mathematics. Geometric language and imagery provide contexts and tools for developing and applying ideas in many other areas of mathematics.

Your work as a teacher of mathematics in these grades calls for a solid understanding of the mathematics that you—and your school, your district, and your state curriculum—expect your students to learn about geometry. Your work also requires you to know how this mathematics relates to other mathematical ideas that your students will encounter in the lesson at hand, the current school year, and beyond. Rich mathematical understanding guides teachers' decisions in much of their work, such as choosing tasks for a lesson, posing questions, selecting materials, ordering topics and ideas over time, assessing the quality of students' work, and devising ways to challenge and support their thinking.

Understanding Geometry

Teachers teach mathematics because they want others to understand it in ways that will contribute to success and satisfaction in school, work, and life. Helping your students develop a robust and lasting understanding of geometry requires that you understand this mathematics deeply. But what does this mean?

It is easy to think that understanding an area of mathematics, such as geometry, means knowing certain facts, being able to solve particular types of problems, and mastering relevant vocabulary. For example, to teach geometry in high school, you are expected to know the properties of several types of transformations. You are also expected to be skillful in determining whether two figures are similar or congruent and use transformations, ratios, and other concepts to explain why a particular relationship holds. Your mathematical vocabulary is assumed to include such terms as *diagonal*, *isometry*, *conjecture*, *symmetry*, and *center*.

Obviously, facts, vocabulary, and techniques for solving certain types of problems are not all that you are expected to know about geometry. For example, in your ongoing work with students, you have undoubtedly discovered that you need not only to know common properties of lines, angles, triangles, quadrilaterals, and circles featured in common theorems but also to be able to follow your students' reasoning as they produce and explore unanticipated conjectures about familiar geometric objects.

It is also easy to focus on a very long list of mathematical ideas that all teachers of mathematics in grades 9–12 are expected to know and teach about geometry. Curriculum developers often devise and publish such lists. However important the individual items might be, these lists cannot capture the essence of a rich understanding of the topic. Understanding geometry deeply requires you not only to know important mathematical ideas but also to recognize how these ideas relate to one another. Your understanding continues to grow with experience and as a result of opportunities to embrace new ideas and find new connections among familiar ones.

Furthermore, your understanding of geometry should transcend the content intended for your students. Some of the differences between what you need to know and what you expect them to learn are easy to point out. For instance, your understanding of the topic should include a grasp of how the study of transformations and matrices at the high school level connects to the study of vector spaces in linear algebra—mathematics that your students might encounter later but do not yet understand.

Other differences between the understanding that you need to have and the understanding that you expect your students to acquire are less obvious, but your experiences in the classroom have undoubtedly made you aware of them at some level. For example, how many times have you been grateful to have an understanding of geometry that enables you to find merit in a student's unanticipated mathematical question or claim? How many other times have you wondered whether you could be missing such an opportunity or failing to use it to full advantage because of a gap in your knowledge?

As you have almost certainly discovered, knowing and being able to do familiar mathematics are not enough when you're in the classroom. You also need to be able to identify and justify or dispute novel claims. These claims and justifications might draw on ideas or techniques that are beyond the mathematical experiences of your students and current curricular expectations for them. For example, you may need to be able to refute the often-assumed, erroneous expectation that transformations of the plane act only on the points that are marked or shown in a figure and not on unmarked points. Or you may need to explain to a student why a line of symmetry of a square represents a reflection that maps the entire square to itself but fixes only two points of the square.

Big Ideas and Essential Understandings

Thinking about the many particular ideas that are part of a rich understanding of geometry can be an overwhelming task. Articulating all of those mathematical ideas and their connections would require many books. To choose which ideas to include in this book, the authors considered a critical question: What is *essential* for teachers of mathematics in grades 9–12 to know about geometry to be effective in the classroom? To answer this question, the authors drew on a variety of resources, including personal experiences, the expertise of colleagues in mathematics and mathematics education, and the reactions of reviewers and professional development providers, as well as ideas from curricular materials and research on mathematics learning and teaching.

As a result, the mathematical content of this book focuses on essential ideas for teachers about geometry. In particular, chapter 1 is organized around four big ideas related to this important area of mathematics. Each big idea is supported by smaller, more specific mathematical ideas, which the book calls *essential understandings*.

Benefits for Teaching, Learning, and Assessing

Understanding geometry can help you implement the Teaching Principle enunciated in *Principles and Standards for School Mathematics*. This Principle sets a high standard for instruction: "Effective mathematics teaching requires understanding what students know and need to learn and then challenging and supporting them to learn it well" (NCTM 2000, p. 16). As in teaching about other critical topics in mathematics, teaching about geometry requires knowledge that goes "beyond what most teachers experience in standard preservice mathematics courses" (p. 17).

Chapter 1 comes into play at this point, offering an overview of the topic that is intended to be more focused and comprehensive than many discussions that you are likely to have encountered. This chapter enumerates, expands on, and gives examples of the big ideas and essential understandings related to geometry, with the goal of supplementing or reinforcing your understanding. Thus, chapter 1 aims to prepare you to implement the Teaching Principle fully as you provide the support and challenge that your students need for robust learning about geometry.

Consolidating your understanding in this way also prepares you to implement the Learning Principle outlined in *Principles and Standards*: "Students must learn mathematics with understanding, actively building new knowledge from experience and prior knowledge" (NCTM 2000, p. 20). To support your efforts to help your students learn about the concepts in this way, chapter 2 builds on the understanding of these operations that chapter 1 communicates by pointing out specific ways in which the big ideas and essential understandings connect with mathematics that students typically encounter earlier or later in school. This chapter supports the Learning Principle by emphasizing longitudinal connections in students' learning about geometry. For example, as students' mathematical experiences expand, the understanding that students develop in middle school about turns, slides, and flips gradually evolves as they progress through high school into an understanding of rotations, translations, and reflections as objects that can themselves be composed, studied, and used as components of geometric arguments.

The understanding that chapters 1 and 2 convey can strengthen another critical area of teaching. Chapter 3 addresses this area, building on the first two chapters to show how an understanding of geometry can help you select and develop appropriate tasks, techniques, and tools for assessing your students' understanding of geometry. An ownership of the big ideas and essential understandings related to geometry, reinforced by an understanding of students' past and future experiences with related ideas, can help you ensure that assessment in your classroom supports the learning of significant mathematics.

Such assessment satisfies the first requirement of the Assessment Principle set out in *Principles and Standards*: "Assessment should support the learning of important mathematics and furnish useful information to both teachers and students" (NCTM 2000, p. 22). An understanding of geometry can also help you satisfy the second requirement of the Assessment Principle, by enabling you to develop assessment tasks that give you specific information about what your students are thinking and what they understand. For example, how would they construct a parallelogram based on different definitions? What do they say changes and what do they say does not change as they look across examples of quadrilaterals that have congruent diagonals? Tasks and questions like these provide insight into how your students understand diagrams, invariance, and definitions and how they use them to develop proof ideas.

Ready to Begin

This introduction has painted the background, preparing you for the big ideas and associated essential understandings related to geometry that you will encounter and explore in chapter 1. Reading the chapters in the order in which they appear can be a very useful way to approach the book. Read chapter 1 in more than one sitting, allowing time for reflection. Take time also to use a dynamic geometry environment or other mathematical tools with tasks that recommend technology use. Absorb the ideas—both big ideas and essential understandings—related to geometry. Appreciate the connections among these ideas. Carry your newfound or reinforced understanding to chapter 2, which guides you in seeing how the ideas related to these operations are connected to the mathematics that your students have encountered earlier or will encounter later in school. Then read about teaching, learning, and assessment issues in chapter 3.

Alternatively, you may want to take a look at chapter 3 before engaging with the mathematical ideas in chapters 1 and 2. Having the challenges of teaching, learning, and assessment issues clearly in mind, along with possible approaches to them, can give you a different perspective on the material in the earlier chapters.

No matter how you read the book, let it serve as a tool to expand your understanding, application, and enjoyment of geometry.

Geometry: The Big Ideas and Essential Understandings

The teaching of geometry in high school can be undertaken as a single integral course or as a set of ideas permeating the entire mathematics sequence in grades 9–12. The approach that we take in this chapter is to consider that geometric big ideas underlie both of these broad approaches to geometry in the high school. So whichever set of commitments you and your school (and perhaps even your district) have made to the teaching of geometry in grades 9–12, the material in this book is worthy of your consideration. Our focus throughout will be Euclidean geometry, almost entirely in the plane, and only on occasion in three dimensions.

Four big ideas and several smaller, more specific essential understandings provide the structure of this chapter. The big ideas and all the associated understandings are identified as a group below to give you a quick overview and for your convenience in referring back to them later. Read through them now, but do not think that you must absorb them fully at this point. The chapter will discuss each one in turn in detail.

Big Idea 1. Working with diagrams is central to geometric thinking.

> **Essential Understanding 1a.** A diagram is a sophisticated mathematical device for thinking and communicating.
>
> **Essential Understanding 1b.** A diagram is a "built" geometric artifact, with both a history—a narrative of successive construction—and a purpose.

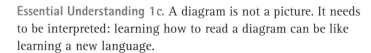

Essential Understanding 1c. A diagram is not a picture. It needs to be interpreted: learning how to read a diagram can be like learning a new language.

Big Idea 2. Geometry is about working with variance and invariance, despite appearing to be about theorems.

Essential Understanding 2a. Underlying any geometric theorem is an invariance—something that does not change while something else does.

Essential Understanding 2b. Invariances are rare and can be appreciated only when they emerge out of much greater variation.

Essential Understanding 2c. Examining the possible variations of an invariant situation can lead to new conjectures and theorems.

Essential Understanding 2d. Geometry is a dynamic study, even if it often appears to be static.

Big Idea 3. Working *with* and *on* definitions is central to geometry.

Essential Understanding 3a. Geometric objects can have different definitions. Some are better than others, and their worth depends both on context and values.

Essential Understanding 3b. Definitions in geometry are of two distinct types: definition *by genesis* (how you can create the object) and definition *by property* (how you can characterize the object in terms of certain features).

Essential Understanding 3c. Building definitions requires moving back and forth between the verbal and the visual.

Big Idea 4. A written proof is the endpoint of the process of proving.

Essential Understanding 4a. Empirical verification is an important part of the process of proving, but it can never, by itself, constitute a proof.

Essential Understanding 4b. Counterexamples are important: individual instances can disprove a conjecture, but they can also lead to modified conjectures.

Essential Understanding 4c. Behind every proof is a proof idea.

Essential Understanding 4d. Geometry uses a wide variety of kinds of proofs.

What's in a Diagram: Big Idea 1

Big Idea 1. *Working with diagrams is central to geometric thinking.*

There is no geometry without diagrams! Diagrams communicate something that verbal language cannot, and vice versa. They also serve to hold still (on paper, in books, on the backboard, in the sand, in the air) the moving pictures of the mind, so that the latter can be considered and argued about. One of the challenges of studying geometry is being able to coordinate the verbal meanings captured by language with the spatial ones represented in diagrams. This challenge extends to coordinating language with the engaging space-time mix of dynamic diagrams (might we call them "dynagrams"?) presented both on computer screens and with physical movement, paper folding, and flexing three-dimensional models. Diagrams are strongly related to visual imagery. Working with and on diagrams can help develop spatial thinking. At the same time, visual imagery is often used in the creation of new diagrams, as well as the interpretation of existing ones.

One diagram is worth a thousand symbols

Essential Understanding 1a. *A diagram is a sophisticated mathematical device for thinking and communicating.*

Just like using vocabulary appropriately, the making and reading of diagrams is something that is learned with practice. Making diagrams can help with the problem-solving process. However, producing diagrams can also promote a better understanding of the particular *grammar* of geometric diagrams—that is, how the diagram structures and renders coherent the meanings that different elements of the diagram are intended to convey. The grammar of geometric diagrams can be quite different from those of other visual illustrations that are encountered both in and out of school.

We begin by offering some diagramming exercises involving the basic objects of high school geometry—lines and circles—and illustrate how such exercises relate to thinking, communicating, and proving. Although you may not find these exercises very challenging mathematically, we nevertheless invite you to engage your hand—and head—in trying them out. As you draw, pay attention to the visual images that you are forming and how that imagery is affected by the new drawings that you create, beginning with Reflect 1.1.

Reflect 1.1

Draw a circle and a line on a piece of paper. How many times do they intersect? How many times *could* they intersect? How many times *must* they intersect?

Which figure did you draw first—the circle or the line? Why? How did this decision affect how you saw things subsequently? Did the prompt determine which you drew first? What if Reflect 1.1 had directed, "Draw a line and a circle..."?

Beginning with your circle, you had to think about how to draw it, what its radius or diameter would be, where its center would lie. Did you anchor your hand at the center and rotate about it, or did your hand perhaps hover above the page, allowing you to keep an eye on the center as you drew? By paying attention to how you are drawing, you can become aware of properties of the circle—properties that will be helpful in your problem-solving process.

Next, with the line, you were faced with a choice of where to place it, of deciding how many different possibilities there might in fact be.

From your drawing alone, after you have drawn both the circle and the line, can you tell which was drawn first? Are the two configurations in figure 1.1 different or the same?

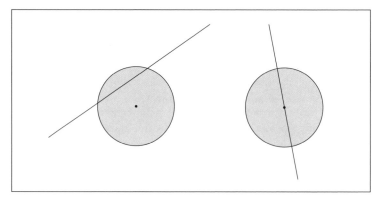

Fig. 1.1. Two possible configurations of a circle and a line intersecting in the same plane

They may seem different, since the configuration on the right has the line passing through the center of the circle—a configuration that may, in some situations, be more special than the one shown on the left. But in both configurations, the line intersects the circle exactly twice (or is it the circle that intersects the line twice?). We might call this line the *secant* line. If we do that, the very name makes the line the cutter. The *secant*, or "cut-line," comes from the Latin verb *seco*, meaning "I cut." In diagramming, the order in which constructions are made may be important, as may be the number of possible intersections.

It is also, of course, possible to have the line not intersect the circle or to have it intersect exactly once. Why cannot there be three intersections? Or four? The process of drawing the lines can support your argument for the impossibility of three or four intersections. Three or more intersections would require going back into the circle after having exiting it, but doing so is impossible if the line is to remain straight.

In drawing the case of one intersection, you are beginning to work with the idea of a *tangent*, or "touch-line," from the Latin verb *tango*, meaning "I touch." In diagramming, working with the tangent is very closely related to the idea of touching once (or perhaps touching twice, but both times in the same place, linked to the algebraic notion of repeated roots). The sequence of diagrams in figure 1.2, which shows the three different types of intersections, also illustrates the visual experiment in which the tangent line to the circle forms one boundary between cases of no intersections and all those of two. In your mind's eye, you might set this sequence of "stills" into motion, with the line moving left (or is the circle the active aggressor, moving to the right, encroaching on the line?). Seeing static diagrams dynamically involves reintroducing the element of time.

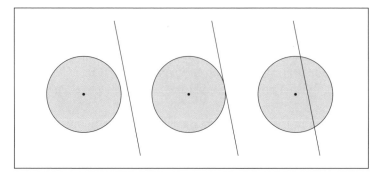

Fig. 1.2. Experimenting by translating the intersecting line

Another diagrammatic experiment involving the tangent line might look like figure 1.3, in which a line passing through a given point on the circumference of the circle can tilt right or left on the radius line, with the middle diagram again showing a boundary or transitional stage, in which the line sits perpendicular to the radius. This boundary case may be communicated propositionally, as a property of the tangent to a circle. Exploring this diagrammatic sequence offers a different way of thinking geometrically. The

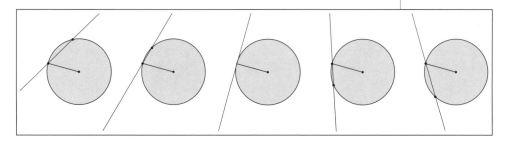

Fig. 1.3. Experimenting by tilting the intersecting line

ordering in time is lurking surreptitiously in the background, arising from a sense of continuous change constrained in specific ways.

These diagrams suggest ways of thinking about why the tangent *must* be at right angles to the radius at the common point of tangency (and equally, why the radius must be at right angles to the tangent). If the radius and line are not perpendicular, the line clearly intersects the circle twice. Thinking about these diagrams dynamically also focuses attention exactly on the key place—namely, the point where the line and the radius intersect (which is the point of rotation of the line).

Seeing the line totter, as it were, on the endpoint of the radius might also lead to thinking about the tangent line in terms of reflectional symmetry. The radius of the circle acts as the line of reflection for the tangent line, so it must be perpendicular to it. Note that one of the root meanings of the word *right* has to do with balance—in the case of *right angle*, the same amount (of angle) on one side as on the other.

As for figure 1.2, our discussion of figure 1.3 exemplifies the way in which we can move *from* the diagram *to* the property. This approach reverses the usual order presented in textbooks of movement *from* the property *to* the illustrative diagram. It helps to build your store of visual imagery, so that the property is not simply a set of words.

We noted in passing that while the diagrams in figure 1.3 are all static, the sequencing of them in the figure may provide a sense of dynamism, as one can imagine the line being tilted progressively from leaning right to leaning left. Figure 1.4 may communicate the dynamism more effectively. As we will discuss in relation to Big Idea 2, reading a geometric diagram sometimes involves being able to see it as involving dynamic variation. That is, we can see the diagram as showing a single thing changing over time, rather than a plurality of different objects all at the same time. Reflect 1.2 invites you to sketch several circles before we return to dynamic variation.

 Big Idea 2

Geometry is about working with variance and invariance, despite appearing to be about theorems.

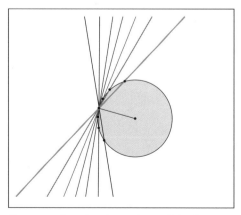

Fig. 1.4. Representing the dynamism of the intersecting line

Reflect 1.2

Illustrate the claim that two circles can intersect zero, one, two, or infinitely many times.

Reflect 1.2 gives the statement of a claim and calls for the use of diagrams for exploring and communicating. You might produce a sequence of diagrams such as those shown in figure 1.5.

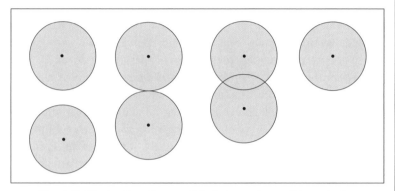

Fig. 1.5. Illustrating the possible intersections of two circles

The sense of motion here is motion in time, but also motion across space. Can you view this diagram symmetrically in terms of two different circles approaching each other and eventually fusing to become one? Does the fact one set of circles is drawn horizontally affect your interpretation? You might also consider what happens to that very sequence if both circles are not the same size, in which case you need to think about how to use the diagrams to represent the full range of possibilities that you perceive. Now you are using diagrams to communicate the variation that is possible in a seemingly simple proposition.

Similar kinds of exercises can be undertaken with any geometric proposition. The goal of diagramming is to develop a sense of both the dependencies and variability of different geometric objects and their possible configurations. In doing so, you provide visual support and inspiration for discursive work. What "story" would you tell about these pictures—a voice-over accompaniment, perhaps, to the silent film of their moving? Why are these the significant way stations on the journey? How might students become more adept at telling diagrammed stories about geometry, especially from a sequence of geometric images that have no verbal captions?

Every diagram tells a story

Essential Understanding 1*b*. *A diagram is a "built" geometric artifact, with both a history—a narrative of successive construction—and a purpose.*

Very often, diagrams are given, pre-made. They are used to illustrate a geometric configuration in terms of which a certain problem is posed. In these cases, how the diagram was created, or why this one and not some other, is never obvious. The accompanying text might provide this information, to a certain degree, but the diagram, by itself, does not. Diagrams seem to be mute. But perhaps we ourselves can get better at "listening" *to* them and at speaking *for* them.

When thinking of diagrams, we can come up with ones as simple as that in figure 1.6a, or more complicated ones, such as that in figure 1.6b (which can be seen as an additional variation on the theme of fig. 1.1, involving a circle, a line, and a second line). Given only the static diagram in figure 1.6a, we cannot be certain whether it is a kite or perhaps simply an arbitrary quadrilateral whose shape on this occasion is "close to" that of a kite, a particular quadrilateral that we will discuss in more detail in a moment.

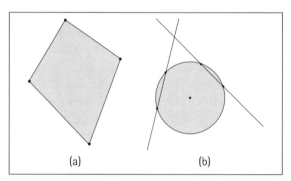

(a)   (b)

Fig. 1.6. Two geometric diagrams of differing complexity

The power of a point theorem holds that for a point P, a circle, and two lines through P, with one intersecting the circle at points A and B, and the other intersecting the circle at points C and D, $AP \cdot BP = CP \cdot DP$.

Just by combining what we assume to be three simple objects in a certain way, figure 1.6b presents a configuration that gives rise to the power of a point theorem. Were the two lines drawn first, with the circle intersecting each one twice? Was the point of intersection of the two lines given, as well as the circle, and then two lines drawn? It is impossible to tell from the diagram. Different backstories are possible, and different narratives that can make a difference. Reflect 1.3 asks for such a story.

Reflect 1.3

What is a possible history for the kite diagram shown in figure 1.6a? Might the diagram have a different history, or many different ones? And might its history depend on the tools that were used to produce it?

Why worry about the history of a diagram? The reason is simple: the story reveals the way in which different parts of the diagram depend on each other. The history of a diagram draws attention to both the givens and the properties that a certain diagram can communicate and signify.

One possible history of figure 1.6a, illustrated in figure 1.7, involves starting with an arbitrary segment, adding another, and then using circles to determine a fourth vertex in such as a way as to construct two sets of adjacent congruent sides. The fourth diagram in the sequence shows the conclusion of the history—the "steady state" for the diagram. This story communicates the idea that a kite can begin with two arbitrary segments connected at one vertex. From there, the kite is completely determined by the intersection of the circles centered at the non-common endpoints of the segments, with radii equal to the segments. So, any time that we see a kite, we might now imagine those two circles there, hovering in the background.

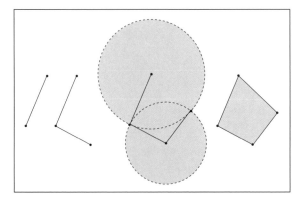

Fig. 1.7. One possible "history" for the kite diagram

Figure 1.8 conveys a different history. Instead of starting with two arbitrary segments, this account starts with one segment, and an adjacent, congruent segment, constructed by using a circle as a tool. The third diagram shows the perpendicular bisector through the common vertex to the segment connecting the two points on the circle. A fourth vertex is constructed on the perpendicular bisector and connected to each of the points of intersection on the circle.

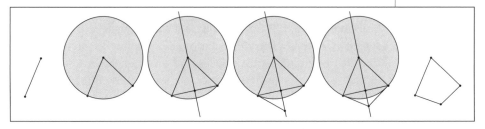

Fig. 1.8. A second possible "history" for the kite

Linking different histories of diagrams for geometric objects is similar to linking different representations of functions. As noted in *Developing Essential Understanding of Functions for Teaching Mathematics in Grades 9–12,* "Links among these different representations are important to studying relationships and change" (Cooney, Beckmann, and Lloyd 2010, p. 78).

The first story leads to a certain range of variation at the outset. Changing the lengths of the sides or the angle at which they meet generates certain families of kites. The second story invites one to consider where that fourth vertex might "land" and, in particular, what happens if it lands *inside* the triangle. This second story leads to exactly the same conclusion as the previous one. In this story, however, the perpendicular bisector tool makes a surprise guest appearance, providing "for free" the second pair of adjacent, congruent sides. The first angle is arbitrary, but it is not until later in the construction that another choice is made—the selection of the point lying on the perpendicular bisector. This choice is not completely arbitrary, because the fourth vertex must also lie on the perpendicular bisector.

Both of these histories involve using basic straightedge and compass tools (or, in a dynamic geometry environment, the line and the circle tools). But the third story, which we now offer in figure 1.9, differs from the previous two, in that the fourth step involves using transformations as tools to make the construction.

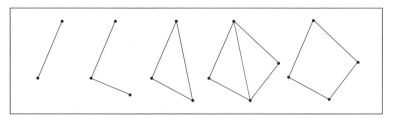

Fig. 1.9. A third possible "history" for the kite

The two initial segments are reflected across the segment that is constructed in the third step and joins their endpoints. Once again, the conclusion is the kite. However, in this case, the mirror line is first and foremost a mirror, rather than before, when it was deployed as a perpendicular bisector. This history draws attention more immediately to the symmetry of the kite than to the fact that the two adjacent segments have the same length.

Visual histories such as we have been examining also all have their associated verbal histories. Reflect 1.4 asks you to consider the story told by a different representation. By using the script view in The Geometer's Sketchpad, it is possible to see a verbal translation of *any* Sketchpad diagram as a sequence of steps, presented as a recipe. The particular one given in Reflect 1.4 shows the kite depending on the selection of three points, but it is only in the reading of the steps that we see when those three specific points are introduced (in this case, in the first two steps) and in which order.

Reflect 1.4

What story of the kite does the following script, or verbal history of steps, tell?

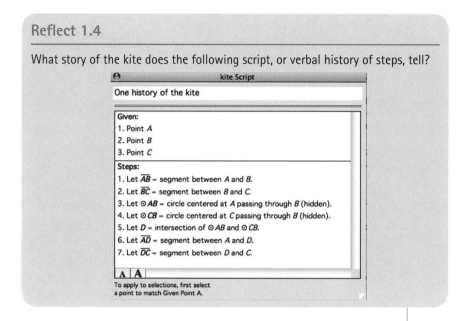

As you worked on the task, you probably drew the objects specified by the steps, creating your own kite (and presumably your kite will be particular to you), thereby moving from the verbal to the visual. This work highlights the differences between the two types of histories. In the diagram, the kite has a specific location, size, and orientation, but not in the script. Little is lost in the diagram by not having labels, but they are essential in the script. The diagram gives one kite; the script could produce any kite. The diagram shamelessly hides its past, while the script tells all. It is evident that each resource has different benefits and drawbacks, and fruitful work is to be done in going back and forth from one to the other.

The challenge of reading diagrams

Essential Understanding 1c. *A diagram is not a picture. It needs to be interpreted: learning how to read a diagram can be like learning a new language.*

In our discussion of Essential Understanding 1*b*, we looked at several diagrams of kites. Each could have been read entirely perceptually—that is, as one particular shape (i.e., as a drawing) rather than as a representation of the idea of *kite* (i.e., as a geometric figure). To illustrate the difference between a drawing and a figure, consider figure 1.10a. Some might call it a "diamond," drawing on a visual comparison between it and other things that they have known to be called diamonds in the past. Calling it a "square," though, involves comparing it with verbal defining properties of the square—namely, that it has four angles that are the same and four sides that are the same (in other words, a square is a regular quadrilateral).

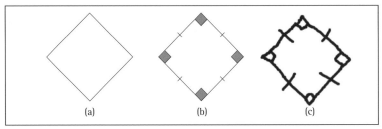

Fig. 1.10. Interpreting diagrams

It may be easier to call figure 1.10a a square if you look at figure 1.10b, since the key symbolic markers communicate some of the properties of the square. These markers may indicate that the diagram is supposed to be seen as a figure. That is, the diagram may be seen as a *general* square, even though it has—and has to have—a particular size, location, and orientation. Indeed, it sometimes happens that a hand-drawn diagram such as figure 1.10c is given. Such diagrams do not appear visually to represent the referent, but they do so "verbally," in the sense that they include symbolic markers that assert the desired properties. Coming to accept figure 1.10c as a square can be a delicate process. Reflect 1.5 presents a different kind of task—one that involves several geometric shapes in a single configuration and presents a greater mathematical challenge.

Reflect 1.5

Given a right triangle *BAC* with right angle at *A*, let *P* be a point on segment *BC* and *I* be a point on segment *AB* such that segment *PI* is perpendicular to segment *AB*, and *J* be a point on segment *AC* such that segment *JP* is perpendicular to segment *AC*. Where should *P* lie on segment *BC* to minimize the length of segment *IJ*? (Adapted from Hollebrands, Laborde, and Sträßer 2008, p. 160.)

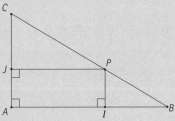

This task would be quite difficult to approach without the given representation. But there are many ways of approaching the diagram. First, we might consider the image as a whole—that is, as a gestalt—and consider globally all the elements and relations of the problem. But since the problem asks for a relationship between *IJ* and *P*, we can approach the diagram more operationally and focus in on a sub-configuration of it—in this case, the rectangle *PIAJ*.

In doing so, we effectively extract the shape *PIAJ* from the whole and see it now as a rectangle in its own right. (Why must it be a rectangle? What is the verbal definition of a rectangle?) Then, to solve the problem, we can go back and forth between the diagram and the statement of the problem, first justifying that *PIAJ* is indeed a rectangle, using the givens, and then, since the task asks for something about the diagonal *IJ*, noting that *IJ* and *AP* have the same length (a known property of rectangles). This might evoke a second diagram, one that shifts our attention from the rectangle *PIAJ* to the related triangles *APB* and *APC*. The question now involves finding how to minimize the length of *AP*, which might lead to our considering the definition of the shortest distance from point *A* to segment *CB*. Returning to the theme of static and dynamic, we can consider figure 1.11 to evoke the idea of moving *P* along *BC* until *AP* attains this minimum distance.

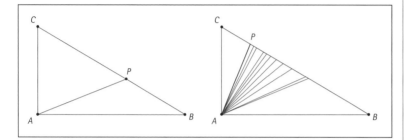

Fig. 1.11. A possible solution to the Reflect 1.5 task

As we can see in this sketch of a solution, movement between the diagram and the verbal statement of the problem is frequent—and sometimes requires the creation of new diagrams. If we stay at the perceptual level, the diagram given in the initial problem may seem entirely distinct from and unconnected to the ones in figure 1.11, and it is likely to be difficult for us to follow this solution to the problem. We must forget about *J* and *I* and attend to the new object, *AP*, which was not invoked by the problem statement at all. It is precisely in drawing the segment *AP* that we can bring it into being (and baptize it "segment *AP*") and begin to treat it as an object that is relevant to the solution. Reading the diagram in Reflect 1.5 therefore involves not only a visual apprehension of the drawing, but also a decoding of the markers (specifically the right-angle markers at *J*, *A*, and *I*). Perhaps more importantly, it also involves the recognition that, though static, *P* has the potential to be anywhere along *BC*. Reflect 1.6 offers a related task, with both of its questions addressing common responses to the original question.

Dynamic reading of a diagram requires visual imagery, which is discussed as a big idea in *Developing Essential Understanding of Geometry for Teaching Mathematics in Grades 6–8* (Sinclair, Pimm, and Skelin 2012).

Reflect 1.6

In Reflect 1.5, when would *J* be at the midpoint of *AC* in order for *IJ* to be minimized? Under what conditions is the location of *P* such that *PIAJ* is a square?

A common first conjecture about the original problem is that *IJ* will be at a minimum when *P* is at the midpoint of *BC*. Another intuitive response is that *P* should be wherever *PIAJ* is a square, perhaps because the square is sometimes a solution to optimization problems in geometry. We can think about a sequence of diagrams in relation to each of these conjectures. In figure 1.12, *P* is the midpoint of *CB*. The length of *AC* varies and the dashed line through *A* is always perpendicular to *CB*. In figure 1.13, *PIAJ* has been fixed to be a square. Again the dotted line through *A* is always perpendicular to *CB*, and again we vary the length of *AC* in the sequence of diagrams.

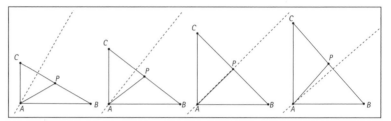

Fig. 1.12. *P* is the midpoint of *CB*

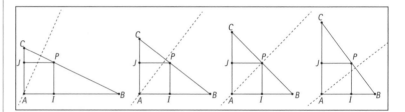

Fig. 1.13. *PIAJ* is a square

The sequence of diagrams in figure 1.13 seems to suggest that the cases of *P* being a midpoint and *PIAJ* being a square amount to the same thing. The diagrams point to a relationship that suggests an "if and only if" conjecture, such as the following:

> The minimum length of *IJ* will occur when *P* is at the midpoint of *BC* if and only if *PIAJ* is a square.

If *P* is at the midpoint, then *CP* = *PB* and ∠*APC* and ∠*APB* are both right angles. We need only to show, for example, that *AJ* = *AI* or *JP* = *PI*, since we already know that *PIAJ* is a rectangle. But triangles *APC* and *APB* are congruent through the side-angle-side (SAS) theorem (since *CP* = *PB*, ∠*APC* and ∠*APB* are both right angles, and *AP* = *AP*), as well as isosceles. Given that *P* cuts *CB* in half, *J* cuts *AC* in half, and *I* cuts *AB* in half, so *AI* = *AJ*. We leave to you the task of showing that if *PIAJ* is a square, then *P* is at the midpoint of *CB*.

When working with geometric diagrams, we sometimes need to be able to see them in different ways—sometimes as drawings of a particular situation, but sometimes as visual statements of generality. Increasingly, with the availability of dynamic visualization tools, we will find it useful to read diagrams temporally, on the screen, as well as statically, on a sheet of paper—as evidenced in both figure 1.12 and figure 1.13, where the sequencing of diagrams suggests some kind of continuous change.

The More It Changes, the More It Stays the Same: Big Idea 2

Big Idea 2. *Geometry is about working with variance and invariance, despite appearing to be about theorems.*

The idea of invariance suggests that something does not change (or changes in a predictable and limited way), against a backdrop of something else that very definitely is changing. Although invariance is a central idea of mathematics in general, it is particularly relevant and important in geometry—and for the teaching of geometry. You have probably encountered students who, when they are shown a shape like that in figure 1.14 and are asked to identify it, refer to it as a "diamond." That might not have surprised you particularly, but if you probed a little further and asked them whether it might not also be a square and they then replied, "It can't be a square, because it's tilted," you might have found the response more perplexing. This example, and many others like it, point to the limited sense that students often have of variance related to geometric figures or constructions. For the students in our example, squares seemingly must have one side parallel to the base of the paper—or the screen, or the horizon (linked to *horizontal*)—to be a square.

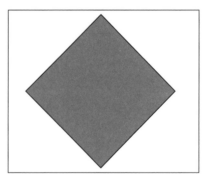

Fig. 1.14. A square or a diamond?

This understanding of square does contain some sense of possible variation—or "dimension of variation," as it is sometimes called (see Leung [2008])—specifically, in the size of the square and even its location (at the top of the paper or in the middle). But it lacks a dimension of variation with regard to its possible orientation *relative to the frame of the page*. In geometry, the scope of reference of the word *square* includes all possible variations that a square can have while still maintaining its defining properties. In this sense, the square is an object of invariance as well, since the properties of congruent (and right) angles and congruent sides are invariant across the range of all squares.

Dynamic geometry software can be particularly powerful in drawing attention to invariance in the midst of variation. Dragging the vertices of a square on the screen can evoke the sense of producing a wide range of squares. And in transforming a shape (e.g., changing the length of the sides, the size of the angles, the location, the orientation), one creates a visual and temporal illustration of "square" in a way that a static example, or even a set of such examples, cannot.

From a geometric point of view, most theorems can be seen as resulting from studies of permitted change that leave some relationship or property invariant. The theorem specifies the specific invariance while also documenting the circumstances under which the invariance remains invariant. For example, changing the shape of a triangle leaves invariant the interior angle sum, *provided that the figure remains triangular and in the plane*. Notice that, in this example, the central and important idea contained in the theorem is about the *invariance* of the angle sum. The particular value of this invariant sum can be found and expressed in terms of either two right angles or 180 degrees, but the actual value matters less than the fact of the invariance. Perhaps we can appreciate the importance of the invariance better by comparing the Euclidean triangle with triangles in spherical or hyperbolic geometry, where the sum of the angles depends on the size of the triangle—and is therefore not at all invariant.

For further discussion of both Euclidean and non-Euclidean geometry, see Henderson and Taimina (2006).

Another example relates to a transversal cutting two parallel lines. No matter how the transversal is positioned across the pair of parallel lines (provided it is not parallel to them), the relationship (in this case, congruence) between related pairs of angles such as the pair shown in figure 1.15a is invariant. In the second configuration (fig. 1.15b), the invariant relationship between the two marked angles is that their angle sum is always (like in a triangle) two right angles.

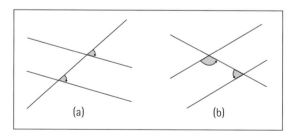

(a)   (b)

Fig. 1.15. Angles with invariant relationships

There are other ways of seeing the implied theorem as exemplifying a study in invariance—different stories told from the diagrams. For example, suppose that you start out with two intersecting lines j and k in the plane, as illustrated in figure 1.16. What happens if you rotate the lines around their point of intersection by 180 degrees?

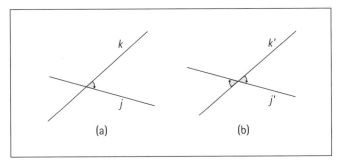

Fig. 1.16. Rotating the angle in (a) by 180 degrees to obtain the angle in (b)

If one assumes that rotation preserves both angles and side lengths, then one can establish that the opposite angles are the same. No matter how those initial lines are placed, rotating them by a half-turn does not change the congruence of the opposite angles And what happens if you translate *j* in the direction of *k*? No matter how you change the magnitude of the translation, the related pairs of angles retain their relationship to each other. In addition to illustrating the importance of invariance in geometry, this transformational approach to justifying the theorem—where the nature of the permitted variation lies in the specific translation—strikes us as quite compelling.

The set of theorems in school geometry related to a transversal cutting a pair of parallel lines also includes the one that two angles such as those shown in figure 1.17a are supplementary (in other words, their sum is invariant, and the invariant sum is two right angles). We can see the theorem about the sum of the angles of any triangle being invariant (and that sum being two right angles) as arising from the previous configuration. To do so, we rotate line *j* around vertex *B* counterclockwise without *j* coinciding with *k*, creating a new point at *C*, the intersection of lines *j* and *l*, and along with it, a triangle, *ABC*. No matter how much or how little we rotate that line, the sum of the angles will remain invariant—with the change in value of the angle at *C* being precisely compensated for by the changing value of the angle at *B*.

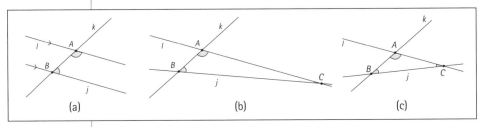

Fig. 1.17. From transversal to triangle by rotating *j* around *B*

In this way, two apparently unrelated configurations (that of the triangle and that of two parallel lines cut by a transversal) and two theorems (that the angle sum of a triangle and the sum of the included angles within the parallels are both invariant and equal to two right angles) can be seen to be very closely related (see fig. 1.18). Indeed, the parallel line–transversal configuration can be seen as a boundary case of a triangle, to use the language of our discussion of Big Idea 1.

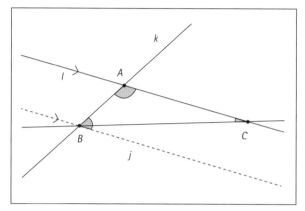

Fig. 1.18. Superimposing the configurations from figure 1.17a and 1.17c

Where geometric theorems come from

Essential Understanding 2a. *Underlying any geometric theorem is an invariance—something that does not change while something else does.*

Without constraints, we would have no theorems. Constraints permit a range of variation from which we can find certain properties and relationships. We have seen the sum of the angles of a triangle in the plane not changing while the triangle changes across its entire range of possible variation, becoming in turn all the possible triangles that it could be. Other examples include the Pythagorean relationship, which identifies an invariance across a range of all possible right triangles. Once again, we note that invariance occurs in other areas of mathematics as well, but in geometry, which in secondary school is most often concerned with the two-dimensional plane, the range of variation involves continuity.

In other domains of school mathematics, the range of variation is often more discrete. For example, theorems and conjectures in elementary number theory are concerned with variation *over the range of whole numbers* (for example, only square numbers have an odd number of factors) or over the range of even numbers greater than 2 (for instance, any even number is a sum of two primes). Consider invariance in relation to transformations in Reflect 1.7.

Reflect 1.7

Generate a list of different types of transformations that you know about. Classify them in terms of their invariances. For example, angles are invariant under dilation and also under reflection.

Geometry is typically thought of as being about working with definitions, theorems, and proofs. However, for several reasons, we claim that it is important to highlight its essence as seeking and working with invariance. One reason relates to the significant role that variation plays in students' conceptions of geometric objects. Another reason relates to the shift in mathematics away from the axiom-driven view of geometry that had prevailed from the writing of Euclid's *Elements* to the later nineteenth century, when the young mathematician Felix Klein decided to characterize geometries not in terms of their underlying axioms but in terms of their changing sets of allowable variations and invariances.

The most restrictive geometry (in terms of giving rise to the greatest number of invariants) is the one based on isometries, where the transformations leave invariant distance (and thus length, perimeter, and area) and angles, as well as parallel and perpendicular lines (see the green *F*'s in fig. 1.19). The next most restrictive geometry includes similarity transformations, where we let go of the invariance of size and instead only require invariance of ratios of distances (ratios of corresponding side lengths) and angles, as well as parallel and perpendicular lines (the black *F* in fig. 1.19). The shearing transformations leave area and parallelism invariant but not distance or angles, or, therefore, perpendicularity. In the most unconstrained geometry, topology, the transformations (such as ones that stretch and pull but do not tear) leave invariant only properties such as the number of holes in a shape or its connectivity. Klein's nesting of geometries is thus essentially about considering what changes and what stays the same under various types of allowable transformations.

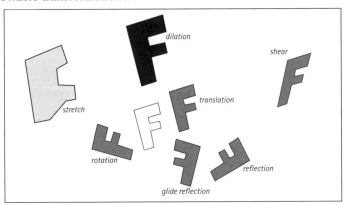

Fig. 1.19. Images under various transformations of the white F

One of the most important tasks in working geometrically involves identifying invariance and, perhaps even more important, identifying things that might be changed to see whether something else stays the same. In our discussion of Essential Understanding 2*a*, we mentioned two cases in which quantities are invariant: the sum of the angles of a triangle and the relationship among the squares on the sides of a right triangle, identified in the Pythagorean theorem. However, this chapter will provide many examples of invariances. Essential Understanding 2*b* underlines the fact that invariances are actually rare, even though this might not seem to be the case for students, who are almost always shown *only* invariances, in the guise of theorems.

Homing in on sameness

Essential Understanding 2*b*. *Invariances are rare and can be appreciated only when they emerge out of much greater variation.*

Our discussion of Essential Understanding 2*b* begins with the task in Reflect 1.8.

> ### Reflect 1.8
>
> Draw or create a triangle. Measure the lengths of its sides. While keeping within the realm of triangles, what could you vary so that something else remains invariant?

The task in Reflect 1.8 is rarely assigned in school, especially when compared with the task of finding the sum of the interior angles of a triangle. However, it provides an opportunity to encounter and struggle with the fact that invariances are rare in geometry. This rarity is, in part, related to value. One might try to see if *anything* remains invariant about the sum of the sides, which many students who have encountered the sum of the angles theorem try first. If that fails, what else one might do? What other invariants might there be?

We might say that if the triangle is obtuse, the side opposite the obtuse angle is always longer than either of the other two sides. Identifying this invariance involves constraining the space of triangles to obtuse ones. But in mathematics, those who state a theorem often want to chase the invariance as widely as possible. So we might do more geometric work by trying to extend this invariance to the full class of all triangles. It is also true in obtuse triangles that the sum of the lengths of the other two sides is greater than the length of the side opposite the obtuse angle. Might this invariance (the sum of two side lengths) be applicable across a wider range of triangles? The Pythagorean theorem can also be seen in this way.

Although the sum of two side lengths of a triangle is always greater than the third side length, when looking at right triangles and squares placed on those the sides, we find that the advantage has disappeared. The sum of the two exactly matches the third. So this "contest" ends in a draw—every time!

But having shifted our attention to squares, what can we say about the relation of squares on sides of non-right triangles? A visual experiment on an acute-angled triangle can convince us that the square on the side opposite the largest angle is always less than the sum of the squares on the other two sides. Similarly, in an obtuse triangle, the square on the side opposite the obtuse angle is always greater than the sum of the squares on the two other sides. This is a qualitative version of the cosine law. Can we be more precise about the size of the difference?

Figure 1.20 shows two different ways of dissecting a specific heptagon constructed from the same starting acute triangle ABC (the corresponding pictures are different if ABC is obtuse). In figure 1.20a, the square on AC is constructed first, and then two copies of the triangle ABC are placed along the sides of that square. Last, two parallelograms are created. In figure 1.20b, the squares on BC and AB are created first, and then two copies of triangle ABC are combined to make a parallelogram, as shown.

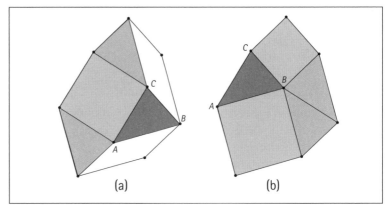

Fig. 1.20. Two ways of decomposing the same heptagon based on the same acute-angled triangle

The claim is that the two heptagons so created are identical. Taking this as given, we can see that each dissection has three copies of the starting triangle. In addition, the one on the left has the square on AC and two parallelograms, whereas the one on the right has the squares on AB and BC. The two white parallelograms have the same area:

$$BC \cdot AC \cdot \cos(ACB)$$

The cosine law for triangles, when compared with the Pythagorean theorem, can be read in terms of a "correction factor"

$(-2 \cdot BC \cdot AC \cdot \cos(ACB))$ equal to the size of the difference to be taken into account.

Notice that when the original triangle ABC is a right triangle, the white parallelograms disappear, the heptagon becomes a pentagon, and we have a proof by dissection of Pythagoras's theorem (see fig. 1.21).

For further discussion of dissection arguments, see *Developing Essential Understanding of Geometry for Teaching Mathematics in Grades 6–8* (Sinclair, Pimm, and Skelin 2012).

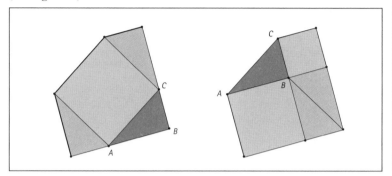

Fig. 1.21. Two ways of decomposing the same pentagon based on the same right triangle ABC

Reflect 1.8 and the subsequent discussion illustrate the way in which geometric work involves a back-and-forth between identifying things that might be varied and looking at whether those variations nevertheless produce any invariances.

Where conjectures come from

Essential Understanding 2c. *Examining the possible variations of an invariant situation can lead to new conjectures and theorems.*

Brown and Walter's (1990) *What-if-not?* problem-posing strategy, which we ourselves have drawn on in our statement of Essential Understanding 2c, provides an effective way of directly changing the constraints of a geometric situation or configuration. In fact, Reflect 1.8 can be seen as an instance of asking what-if-not? regarding the Pythagorean theorem by posing the question, "What if the triangle does not have to be right-angled?" Brown and Walter offer many other variations on the Pythagorean theorem set up by what-if-not? questions, including "What-if-it-is-not squares constructed on the three sides, but circles, regular hexagons, or rectangles?" "What-if-it-is-not a triangle at all?" and, "Is there a relationship between the squares constructed on the four sides of a (some, any) quadrilateral?"

We can generate all of these what-if-not? questions by looking at the statement of the Pythagorean theorem, and at the nouns in particular, and then considering how they might be varied, one by one. The theorem might be read aloud a number of times, each time forcefully emphasizing a different word that might be changed, not only to hear the particular conditions of the Pythagorean theorem, but also, through the specific emphasis on a chosen word, to think about ways in which that item might be altered to provide new investigations in mathematical possibility. Notice the words that matter in Reflect 1.9.

Reflect 1.9

"What-if-not?" the following statement: The midpoints of a triangle form another triangle similar to the original one, but with one-fourth its area.

In this case, the statement of invariance (that the midpoints always form a new triangle of a certain shape and size relative to the triangle that gave rise to it) depends on the two nouns *triangle* and *midpoint*. What if we did not use the midpoints? What are some alternatives? This is the stage at which we are working to generate variation—we are varying the idea of the midpoint. One option would be to use the "$1/3$ point" or the "$1/4$ point." Figure 1.22 shows an example using the $1/3$ point. As it turns out, the inner triangle is no longer similar to the original one; however, its area is nevertheless exactly $1/3$ that of the original. With the $1/4$ case, the ratio of the areas is not $1/4$, as we might have hoped, but almost $1/2$.

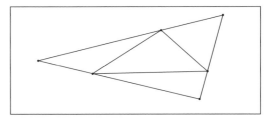

Fig. 1.22. The "1/3 point" triangle

An invariance has been lost, but another conjecture might be lurking: when we use the "$1/n$ point" to form an inner triangle in this way, as n increases, the ratio of the areas of the triangles also increases. So we have found a new conjecture, but it has also suggested a more global conjecture about the relationship between the "$1/n$ point" triangle and the ratio of its area to that of the original triangle. The continued increase of the ratio certainly makes sense when one considers that for very large n, the inner triangle will almost coincide with the original one, thus tending toward a ratio of 1:1.

We will explore this situation further in our discussion of Essential Understanding 4c. However, for now, we return to the prompt in Reflect 1.9, which was to what-if-not? (now it is a verb!)

Essential
Understanding 4c

*Behind every proof is
a proof idea.*

the statement about the midpoint triangle. Another possible variation would involve varying the word *triangle*—what if we did not
have a triangle but instead a quadrilateral? Could we find a midpoint quadrilateral?

In drawing an example of such a case (see fig. 1.23), we encounter a new question that did not arise in the case of the triangles—namely, that there are two possible midpoint quadrilaterals
(and even though some might not want to call fig. 1.23b a quadrilateral, there is at least some work for us to do in deciding *how* the
midpoints are to be joined). As with the variation of the midpoint
exercise, the variation of the triangle exercise can lead not only to
the quadrilateral, but to any polygon (and the numerous ways of
joining the points), therefore potentially leading to a new invariance
against the variation of the number of sides. For an investigation of
invariances involving a midpoint pentagon, see Zbiek (1996).

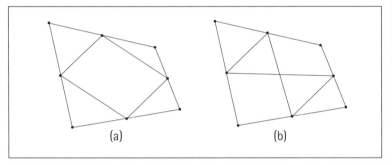

(a)   (b)

Fig. 1.23. Two different midpoint quadrilaterals from the same
starting quadrilateral?

High school geometry tends to emphasize invariances that are
related to length, area, or angle (and the associated congruences and
similarities). However, symmetry is also a property that can be varied or examined for possible invariance. For example, an isosceles
triangle can be seen as having as an invariant the fact that two sides
are always the same length (or two angles are always the same size).
But from the point of view of symmetry, an isosceles triangle also always has one line of reflectional symmetry as an invariant property.
Again, from the perspective of symmetry, an equilateral triangle has
three rotational symmetries as an invariant property.

With respect to the midpoint quadrilateral, we can also use
symmetry to generate new conjectures. For example, if the initial
quadrilateral is a rectangle, which has two reflectional symmetries,
then the midpoint quadrilateral is a rhombus, which also has two
reflectional symmetries. This could lead to a conjecture that the
midpoint quadrilateral has the same number of reflectional symmetries as the original quadrilateral.

Moving to stay the same

Essential Understanding 2d. Geometry is a dynamic study, even if it often appears to be static.

 Essential Understanding 1b

A diagram is a "built" geometric artifact with both a history—a narrative of successive construction—and a purpose.

 Essential Understanding 1a

A diagram is a sophisticated mathematical device for thinking and communicating.

Essential Understanding 2d asserts that although the study of geometry often appears to be static, it is in fact dynamic. If this claim surprises you at first, it may well be because the tools with which you do geometry and the media through which you "read" geometry are static ones. Indeed, there is not much dynamism in diagrams such as those in figure 1.23. Of course, as indicated in Essential Understanding 1b, the process of creating a diagram is certainly dynamic. Furthermore, as shown in Essential Understanding 1a, ways of thinking with and through diagrams can also be quite dynamic.

Similarly, in many of the ways that we have of talking and, especially, writing about geometry, the dynamism is often lost. We may say, "A square is a rectangle," when we mean, "A square is a special type of rectangle." Or, working in a dynamic geometry environment with a constructed rectangle, we could also say, "You can drag any rectangle into a square"—a statement that evokes the range of possible rectangles. Our discussion of Big Idea 2 has focused on illustrating the ways in which geometric theorems, often stated in static language, are actually statements about variance and invariance. We have also argued that thinking of theorems in terms of the variances and invariances that they embody increases our ability to understand and produce them.

As it turns out, many of the variances and invariances that turn up in school geometry involve the kinds of continuous transformations that are well supported by DGEs. Starting at the most basic level, we can think of definitions as being statements about variance and invariance. For example, the triangle is a polygon with three sides that are joined pairwise at their endpoints and remain connected no matter where their vertices happen to be (unless they happen to be collinear). The dragging of a triangle by its vertices or edges (mentally or on the screen) embodies exactly this dynamic definition. Reflect 1.10 extends the discussion to a different dynamic definition.

Reflect 1.10

Provide a definition of a parallelogram in terms of its variances and invariances.

When constructing a shape—say, a parallelogram—in a DGE, we undertake the sequence of construction steps that we could carry out with a compass and straightedge, invoking properties of the shape—in the case of the parallelogram, opposite pairs of sides parallel. However, unlike the compass-and-straightedge environment, a DGE also permits us to follow up the construction with what is known as a "drag test." The goal of a drag test, in which one drags various components of the construction, can often be to make sure that the construction is not "messed up"–the phrase suggested by Healy and colleagues (1994)–that is, checking that it does not break down when pieces of it are varied. In this sense, a dragged construction provides a sense of the scope of the variation that a construction can have.

In the case of the parallelogram (see fig. 1.24), the dragged figure illustrates the properties that have to remain invariant–two opposite sides being parallel, the opposite angles being equal, the opposite sides being equal–while others, including the lengths of the sides and the sizes of the angles, may vary.

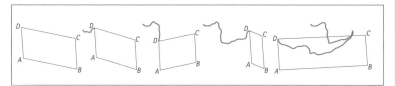

Fig. 1.24. A parallelogram undergoing a "drag test" with vertex *D* dragged along the colored path

The advantage of a dynamic definition lies not simply in providing a range of specific examples for a given class of shapes, but also in offering support for the process of conjecturing. So, for example, when attending to the diagonals of a parallelogram, we may not notice, from a single drawing, that they always bisect each other. It can be difficult to see this as a conjecture–the single drawing offers no evidence of invariance. But once the parallelogram with its diagonals drawn in is dragged, the invariance of this relationship almost pops out. Dragging acts like a magnifying glass that draws attention to invariance for everyone to see. Reflect 1.11 capitalizes on the potential of dragging.

Reflect 1.11

Construct a circle and its diameter. Choose a point on the circumference, label it *P*, and join it to the endpoints of the diameter. What do you see? Drag point *P* on the circumference. Now what do you see?

In all likelihood, you do not immediately see that there is (indeed, must be) a right angle in the triangle at *P*. But when you drag

it, what you do see is that the angle does not change (this might be easier to "see" if you measure the angle!). This is the invariance that is crucial. Once you see that the angle does not change, you can set about finding out what it is. Once you know that the angle is invariant, the symmetric, "isosceles" position, shown in figure 1.25, immediately declares the angle to be a right angle.

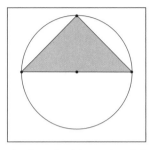

Fig. 1.25. An inscribed isosceles right triangle

Now, perhaps you knew that is was a right angle when you first looked because you were familiar with the underlying theorem. But for students *who do not already know what to look at or for*, the dynamic variation of the point on the circumference first draws their attention to the presence of the theorem. If you worked in a DGE to investigate the midpoint quadrilateral that we suggested earlier as a variation on the midpoint triangle in Reflect 1.9, you may not have noticed that this derived quadrilateral had to be a parallelogram until you dragged the original quadrilateral around.

The particular dynamic variation offered in DGEs is a continuous one, though it is represented on the screen by discrete points because of the way in which computer graphics are produced. The point on the circumference does not just randomly move around; it moves in a continuous fashion, echoing the continuous movement of your hand on the mouse. Similarly, with the triangle, when you drag the vertex of the triangle, the transformation is continuous. This enables the user to see the multiple triangles created through dragging *as one single object.*

Continuity is important to perception, but it also enables us to preserve a geometric focus when working with shapes. Consider our earlier investigation of the shape formed by connecting the midpoints of a triangle. We then turned the question of the midpoint into one of the 1/3 point and the 1/4 point. We shifted to the numerical register. But the continuous nature of dragging enables a different kind of approach. Take any point P along one side AB of the triangle, and then two points on BC and CA, respectively, that lie at the same relative spot along those segments as P does on AB (see fig. 1.26). This always produces a new triangle, but one that we can continuously drag to see what invariances there might be with respect to the new triangle while we vary P continuously.

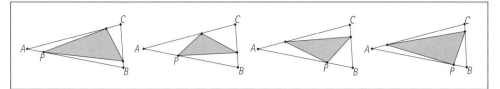

Fig. 1.26. Varying point *P*

Instead of considering each of the cases $1/2$, $1/3$, and $1/4$ as discrete and separate, continuous transformation enables us to see a continuous range of possible positions for *P* going from *A* to *B* and to mobilize the variation to seek new invariances. In particular, it is clear from figure 1.26 that as *P* moves from *A* to *B*, the new triangle goes from occupying all of the original triangle to occupying its minimum amount at the midpoint, to occupying all of it again. A certain symmetry is involved on either side of the midpoint. The dynamic, continuous variation thus permits a degree of generalization that a discrete approach does not so readily support.

In our discussion of Essential Understanding 2*d*, we have focused on the effect of dragging and dynamism on the way in which we think about particular shapes and the way in which we produce conjectures. When students begin to prepare proofs, they are likely to follow the ideas implied by their exploratory work in a DGE. In our discussion of Big Idea 4, where we focus on the relationship between conjectures and proofs, we will return to the topic of dynamic geometry to discuss the way in which the use of a DGE can assist in the process of moving from conjecture to proof.

Big Idea 4

A written proof is the endpoint of the process of proving.

How to Define Your Terms: Big Idea 3

Big Idea 3. *Working* with *and* on *definitions is central to geometry.*

An interesting account of an interaction between a geometry teacher and a student concerning geometric definitions comes from late eighteenth-century France. The teacher was a noted geometer, Gaspard Monge, and the student was Joseph Fourier, later to become a famous mathematician in his own right. Fourier was apparently critical in class of the textbook definition of *straight line*—the classic definition by property attributed to Archimedes—namely, that a straight line is the path of shortest distance between any two points that lie on it.

Fourier proposed an alternative definition, using the idea of a locus subject to a specific length constraint: a straight line consists of those points that are equidistant from three fixed points in space. He related this definition to the definition of a plane as a set of points equidistant from two fixed points and a sphere (or circle) as those points equidistant from one fixed point.

We are fortunate to have Monge's response to his student's proposal, a few excerpts of which we include here:

> Citizen, ... The definition of the straight line you have given is rigorous. The analogy you have noticed between this definition and that which could be made for the plane, the circle and the sphere is very striking. Permit me to make some further comments.

> The notions you invoke in your definition are more complicated than the line you want to define. They assume a familiarity with geometry that could not have been acquired without the notion of a straight line. Certainly in order to define some type of object in geometry a property must be found that applies to the very object of that type and only to such objects. The chosen property should be the simplest and easiest to conceive.

Monge gives an example and then resumes:

> It is not even sufficient that the defining property be simple and easy to conceive. If possible it must—above all in geometry—be able to offer an image. For instance, suppose the straight lines were able to be defined as follows. Consider an object turning about two of its points like a block of wood turning on a lathe. Most of the points of the object will describe circles of various sizes. But some points will not change position during the motion. The set of such points forms a straight line. Such a definition would not be sufficiently simple because of the ideas of rotation that are used and because of

the difficulty of imagining where the invariant points might lie. The definition does not show a straight line. It fails—despite the concrete example—because it does not offer an image of the line at all. (Fourier and Monge 1795/1883, pp. 139–41)

Reflect 1.12 invites you to consider Monge's response to his student's proposal more closely.

Reflect 1.12

Review Monge's response to Fourier's proposed definition. Identify his criteria for a good definition in geometry, and consider whether you agree with them.

A great deal is going on in this interchange. Monge is offering his wisdom about definitions in geometry and how they *should* work. In terms of the big ideas in this chapter, we can see that he is drawing on the idea of invariance and that of motion, as discussed in connection with Big Idea 2. Even more significant, he is claiming that a good definition in geometry should offer an image. Mathematician Yuri Manin once observed, "A good proof is one that makes us wiser" (1977, p. 51). Following mathematician René Thom, who remarked on the Greek origin of the word *theorem* and its connection to "vision" (1971, p. 697), we might declare that "a good theorem is one that communicates its vision." Following Monge, we would like to propose that a good definition is one that educates our imagination (and, following Gattegno [1984], our awareness).

Big Idea 2

Geometry is about working with variance and invariance, despite appearing to be about theorems.

It is interesting to consider whether Monge's reception of his student's suggestion would have been different had Fourier stayed in the plane and proposed defining a straight line as the locus of points equidistant from two fixed points. Try working on the constrained locus task in Reflect 1.13 with a group of colleagues.

Reflect 1.13

In a large space, have everyone move to a spot that satisfies a particular locus constraint. For example, have two colleagues act as fixed focal points while constraining everyone else to be twice as far from one point as from the other. What is the locus? Try other combinations of fixed elements and constraints.

The task in Reflect 1.13 will enable you and the others in your group to *feel* the constraint as an actual physical restriction, limiting the positions at which you may place yourselves. The participatory physical activity can lead to conjectures about the shape of the path, which the members of your group might then explore on paper.

The type of definition proposed by Fourier for a line is quite common in some later accounts of conic sections (e.g., by

Apollonius; see Fauvel [1987, pp. 20–27]). A parabola can be defined as the locus of those points equidistant both from a point (the *focus*) and a line (the *directrix*). An ellipse is the locus of those points the sum of whose distances from two fixed points (the *foci*) is constant. Reflect 1.14 offers an opportunity to pursue this line of thinking in an exercise that serves as a transition to our discussion of Essential Understanding 3*a*.

Reflect 1.14

By carrying out a what-if-not? analysis of the definitions of a parabola and an ellipse provided in the preceding paragraph, what other related curves can you create? How do these definitions relate to the more contemporary way of specifying curves by equations involving *x* and *y*? How do these definitions relate to definitions suggested by the term *conic section*?

Definitions are tools for geometric investigation

Essential Understanding 3*a*. *Geometric objects can have different definitions. Some are better than others, and their worth depends both on context and values.*

To see how the definitions that are used for geometric objects can vary and influence the way in which we think about related objects, we offer a case study. It reveals some of the choices that must be made in defining even elementary objects. It also points to the important role that language—and etymology in particular—can play in drawing attention to certain features of the objects.

Case Study 1: Angle
Our choice for an initial exploration may surprise you:

> How many angles are there in a triangle?

We doubt that you have actually ever considered this as a mathematical question before. But various possibilities ensue.

The first is to argue from the very name itself. Surely "triangle" names the fact that the figure has to have three angles—otherwise, at the very least, it would be a terrible choice of name that surely by now someone would have changed. In the sixteenth century, Englishman Robert Record wanted English mathematical terminology to have Anglo-Saxon rather than Greco-Roman roots. Yet, even Record used *triangle*, although he wanted to call equilateral triangles "likesides."

A Record-like name for a triangle could be "threeside." Then at least the question, "How many angles are in a threeside?" might pose a bit of challenge. Though surely, you might say, there is a general

result that there are *n* angles in any *n*-sided figure, of which this is
just a simple special case. (We have never seen this claim presented as
a theorem in any geometry textbook. What might a proof of it look
like?) This could be an interesting question to pursue another time.

A second argument involves pointing at and counting on a generic image of a triangle: "All triangles look something like this, so
since there are three angles here...." An alternative possibility might
be based on labeling vertices: "Surely there are as many vertices as
angles as sides in any *n*-sided figure: triangles can always be labeled
A, *B*, *C*, and there are three ways of "pointing at" the angles: *ABC*,
BCA, and *CAB*."

One counterargument might be to say, "But what about angle
CBA, angle *ACB*, and angle *BAC*?" Gesturing at angle *CBA* feels different from gesturing at angle *ABC*. To which you might well respond,
"But they are the same as their counterparts in the original list; see,
angle *ABC* is congruent to angle *CBA*," and so on. But if we think of
an angle as a *turning* (one of the essential understandings about angle,
for sure), then no, they are not the same. Angle *ABC* and angle *CBA*,
for example, are opposite turnings, one to the other. So that would
make six angles, not three, in a triangle. And further, we might think
that *ABC* labels two different angles, one "inside" the triangle—the
interior angle (which in a triangle can be acute or obtuse)—and one
"outside" it—the *exterior angle* (which in a triangle is always reflex. So
that would make six, or even twelve, angles for every triangle.

When problems of counting arise in mathematics, it is important to know what counts as one of the things to be counted, so
that all the items can be properly counted. To know what counts,
we are going to need a definition of *angle*. We then can refer to the
definition to determine whether two angles are the same or not and
also whether outside, or reflex, angles count as angles in a triangle.
But notice that whichever definition we settle on, we already have
a desire—a criterion, perhaps—for a good definition for angle: that
is, when we apply the definition to a triangle, it should yield the
answer, "A triangle has three angles." Reflect 1.15 poses questions
about your textbook's definition.

See Netz (1998)
for more on dia-
grams and the
significance of
naming vertices with
letters in ancient
Greek geometry.

Reflect 1.15

We have a number of different choices for the definition of angle. What definition
does your textbook use, if it gives one? If not, locate one or two that do. Using a
textbook definition, how many angles are there in a triangle?

The situation in case study 1 is quite common with definitions in mathematics, where distinct choices are made—choices that
may have different mathematical consequences—and test cases are
used where the desired answer is already known. Other geometric

examples include whether to use "exactly one" or "at least one" in definitions of certain figures—for instance, the trapezoid. Different authors may require "exactly one pair" of opposite sides of a trapezoid to be parallel (with the result that a parallelogram is not a trapezoid, *by definition*). Others prefer "at least one pair" of opposite sides parallel (whereby a parallelogram *would* be a type of trapezoid). Similarly, a kite is a quadrilateral with two pairs of adjacent sides equal. If the definition allows these two pairs of side lengths to be the same length, then a rhombus can be included as a type of kite. If these pairs of lengths must be different, then a rhombus is not a kite.

In our discussion of the definition of a triangle, we used other geometric words that also require definition, such as *angle*. The key dynamic notion of angle is that of turning; human elbow joints have the right qualities for modeling this notion. In a DGE, select a line segment, and choose one end of it as the point of rotation and rotate about it through a certain amount. When we see an angle as dynamic motion, we face a decision about clockwise or counterclockwise rotation (the computer demands it), whereas when we see an angle as static (as in a conventional drawing of a triangle on the page or a blackboard), that tool trace is no longer apparent.

Given two intersecting lines—say, in The Geometer's Sketchpad—one can "gesture" the angle between them by dragging the marker tool *from* one line segment (or ray) *to* the other. This angle, like the gesture, will have a direction (clockwise or counterclockwise) indicated by an arrow. The arrow is a residual trace of the motion and the tool that is being used in the background to generate the angle. Thus, angles in Sketchpad are always directed and are measured either between 0 and 180 (degrees) or between –180 and 180 (directed degrees)—see figure 1.27. The tracing out of the angle draws attention to the fact that part of the notion of angle is the region swept out in going from one line segment to the other—a description that might suggest another possible definition of angle, by the way (an angle is a region of the plane determined by two rays with a common endpoint). In geometry in general, the difference between a polygon and a polygonal region is widely ignored. Talking about "the area *in* a triangle," as compared with "the area *of* a triangle," is a case in point.

See Developing Essential Understanding of Geometry for Teaching Mathematics in Grades 6–8 (Sinclair, Pimm, and Skelin 2012) for a discussion of the relationship between tool traces and geometric objects.

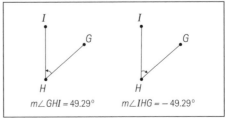

Fig. 1.27. Directed angles and measures in The Geometer's Sketchpad

In DGEs, behind the implementation of tools to construct an angle lies a definition of angle—one that can be inferred from the way in which an angle is both specified and measured by the user. To measure an angle in Sketchpad, one can either select the three points, taken in order, that form the angle (in much the same way that one labels an angle at B, say, with ABC), or one can select the two segments or rays (j and k) that specify the angle (these must have a common endpoint). Therefore, two definitions of angle are operative in Sketchpad. The first defines an angle in terms of three points, given in order. The second defines an angle in terms of two segments or rays with a common endpoint.

Two general facts about definition emerge from this example. The first is that even—or perhaps especially—with apparently straightforward notions such as angle, attempts to define what they are bring us up against unwieldy complexity or unwanted inclusions or desired exclusions. For example, if we use the definition of an angle as three points given in order, then we should include as a quadrilateral the polygon shown in figure 1.28 (which occurs as a border example between concave and convex quadrilaterals).

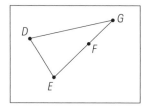

Fig. 1.28. A quadrilateral?

The second fact is that in our attempts to pin down what an angle is to be, our provisional definitions become more and more intricate. With the "two rays meeting at a point" definition, there is only one point, so how are angles to be labeled? (And triangles do not have any rays in them, so do they have no angles?) With the "two segments joined at a point" definition, we at least have three points, but we must still consider the order of the segments. Considering either the order of the points or of the segments may direct attention too far away from the central feature of the image of the concept of angle.

What about the following tentative definition of angle: An angle is an equivalence class that consists of all pairs of line segments or rays with a common endpoint that can be mapped one to another by a composition of isometries. This is similar to the way in which rational numbers can be defined as classes of equivalent fractions. There, a/b is equivalent to c/d, provided that $ad - bc = 0$ and $bd \neq 0$. For example, $11/33$, $30/90$, $1/3$, and $12/36$ all belong to the same equivalence class; hence, all belong to the same rational number. It is helpful that we have two terms in common usage, *fraction* and

See *Developing Essential Understanding of Rational Numbers for Teaching Mathematics in Grades 3–5* (Barnett-Clarke et al. 2010) for a discussion of relationships between fractions and rational numbers.

rational number, to distinguish elements of the equivalence class from the equivalence class itself. However, common usage speaks about "equivalent fractions" rather than "an equivalence class of fractions." Neither of these comments about common parlance applies in the case of angles, as you will see below.

In the angle case, two pairs of line segments or rays with a common endpoint are equivalent if, with the common endpoints superimposed, a sequence of isometries will superimpose both pairs of line segments or rays. This means, as illustrated in figure 1.29a (where all the angles shown belong to the same equivalence class), that either or both of the two line segments can be long, short or virtually infinite, but they can also be of different lengths, and, of course, they can face in different directions.

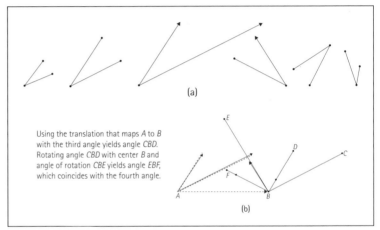

Using the translation that maps *A* to *B* with the third angle yields angle *CBD*. Rotating angle *CBD* with center *B* and angle of rotation *CBE* yields angle *EBF*, which coincides with the fourth angle.

Fig. 1.29. Members of the same equivalence class—therefore, the same angle

To test whether two angles are the same, translate the vertex of one angle to the vertex of the other angle and then use a rotation to superimpose one side of one angle onto a side of the other. If the other two sides also align (or a simple reflection about the common side achieves this), then the two angles are the same. Figure 1.29b illustrates a translation and rotation that maps the third angle to the fourth angle in figure 1.29a.

But is this definition remotely workable in a school setting or textbook—or even comprehensible? What is worse, even with this intricate and sophisticated definition, any triangle still has six or twelve angles. The definition does not resolve the issue of *directed* angles, nor does it take care of the fact that we do not know which of the two angles is supposed to be formed by two segments or rays meeting at a point. One conclusion is that we need to talk more specifically about the *interior angles* of a figure (although given a very complex many-sided polygon, deciding which angle at a given vertex is inside or outside the polygon can be a very challenging question to answer mathematically).

Following Monge, we might add an additional requirement for a definition that is useful for teaching—namely, that it should afford a comprehensible image of the object being defined. For example, the definition of a quadrilateral as a four-sided polygon does little to evoke images, the diversity of instances that fall under it. Finally, images that we have of concepts reside in the mind; they are both dynamic and flexible, whereas definitions in formal mathematics are static and fixed.

However, logician Gottlob Frege's (1884/1960, p. xviii) admonition, "Never let us take a description of the origin of an idea for a definition," is worth bearing in mind. Yet, these cautionary words point to the fact that definitions are seldom starting points, despite their being placed at the start of discussions in many mathematics textbooks (and in mathematics research papers). A workable geometric definition is often the endpoint of back-and-forth negotiations between verbal formulations and a collection of drawn or imagined examples and counterexamples.

Two means of defining

Essential Understanding 3b. *Definitions in geometry are of two distinct types: definition* by genesis *(how you can create the object) and definition* by property *(how you can characterize the object in terms of certain features).*

With the compass—or, perhaps, the forearm—in mind, one can also define an angle as the region swept out by the rotation of the compass—or of the forearm. In the distinction offered by mathematical historian George Molland (1976) between definition *by genesis* and definition *by property*, this would be a definition *by genesis*, which involves saying *what needs to be done* to create the object. This type of definition is in contrast to a definition *by property*, which lists the properties that completely characterize the object (see Monge's description of a definition at the beginning of our discussion of Big Idea 3). The definitions of angle that we offered in our treatment of Essential Understanding 3a—namely, that an angle is defined by three points given in order or by two line segments or rays having a common endpoint—are both definitions by property, since they serve to specify an angle in terms of objects (points) or relations (the common point relating two lines) as properties that the angle must have to be called an angle. The tentative definition of angle as an equivalence class accentuates the properties of an angle while providing no sense of how one might actually create one.

In a glance at the history of geometry, we see Hero's and Euclid's different definitions of a circle. Hero's definition perfectly describes the action of a compass (or a string fixed at one end with a marker at the other):

> A circle is the figure described when a straight line, always remaining in one plane, moves about one extremity as a fixed point until it returns to its first position. (Quoted in Bartolini Bussi and Boni [2003, p. 17].)

Hero's dynamic, mechanical, and procedural approach (saying what you have to do to create a circle—to bring one into being) contrasts with the definition given by Euclid, for whom the compass has already become a mental tool:

> A *circle* is a plane figure contained by one line such that all the straight lines falling upon it from one point among those lying within the figure are equal to one another. (Quoted in Fauvel and Gray [1987, p. 101].)

The definition of a circle offered by Hero is a definition by genesis, which includes active verbs that describe what to do. By contrast, the Euclidean counterpart is a definition by property, describing the essential property of constant radius from a given center. Definitions by genesis are more clearly related to the tools that are associated with bringing the objects into being and are also very frequently the more transparent initial definitions to offer to students.

As the transition from drawing arm to compass revealed, a definition by genesis can often leave its trace in definitions by property. Much is to be learned about geometric objects by comparing the two types of definitions of a given object or by excavating from a definition by property what an underlying definition by genesis might have been. Diagramming is one way of doing this: when creating diagrams of quadrilaterals, we could easily invoke a definition by genesis—for example, making four line segments meet end to end. But there are other ways in which we could define different types of quadrilaterals by genesis. Consider the rectangle as a line segment moving uniformly perpendicularly to itself. Or a parallelogram as a line segment moving uniformly in a skew direction to itself. Shifting to three dimensions, consider the sphere as the rotation of a semicircle around its diameter.

Having discussed some essential understandings about definitions per se, and their relation to the objects they define, we turn our attention next to the roles of definitions in geometric problem solving, and we present a case study in which we focus more specifically on the process through which definitions are built, picking up on the comment that we made in relation to Frege's admonition never to confuse definitions with descriptions about origins.

The marriage of word and image

Essential Understanding 3c. *Building definitions requires moving back and forth between the verbal and the visual.*

Eisenstein (1983) reports on the challenge faced by eleventh-century geometers who were trying to understand the idea of interior angle in the absence of diagrams in texts: "The most learned men in Christendom engaged in a fruitless search to discover what Euclid meant when referring to interior angles" (p. 296). The quotation highlights the way in which definitions and imagery are intertwined—a interrelationship that we elaborate in the case study that follows.

Case Study 2: Defining a quadrilateral

There are many ways of defining quadrilaterals—some much more familiar than others. Reflect 1.16 offers you an opportunity to consider your own definition of a quadrilateral.

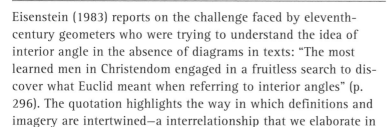

Reflect 1.16

Formulate your own definition of a quadrilateral. Be sure to test it with a range of examples and non-examples (figures that you are quite sure you do not want your definition to include). Do you have any boundary figures—configurations that you are not sure whether to include or not?

What follows is a recounting of our own process of working.

Definition 1: A quadrilateral is a four-sided polygon.

Criticism 1: But what is a polygon? Does it include figures in three dimensions?

Definition 2: (Choosing to respond to the second question in criticism 1) A quadrilateral is a four-sided polygon in a plane.

Criticism 2: I still do not know what a polygon is.

Background definition: A polygon is a planar figure made up of three line segments (edges) or more, joined in pairs only at endpoints.

Criticism 3: What about line segments that cross each other?

Response: No, that would be like two triangles stuck together. Further, we would not know how to make sense of the sum of the interior angles anymore. And what is more, it would then have at least six angles. So...

Definition 3: A quadrilateral is a four-sided polygon in the plane with none of the edges intersecting each other, except at the vertices.

Criticism 4: What about collinear edges?

Response: No, that would be a triangle. We are happy to have a square as a special case of a rectangle but not to have a triangle as a special case of a quadrilateral. Otherwise, the various sets of polygons with different numbers of sides would overlap. So...

Definition 4: A quadrilateral is a four-sided polygon in a plane with none of the edges intersecting each other except at the vertices and none of the edges collinear with each other.

Criticism 5: What about the situation in which one angle is reflex (see fig. 1.30)?

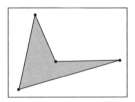

Fig. 1.30. Concave quadrilateral

Response: We do not mind a concave quadrilateral. We will live with a singularity when passing between concave and convex quadrilaterals. We stick with definition 4. For now.

Note that in thinking about the original definition, the examples that initially came to mind did not include crossing, collinearity, or concavity. However, the original definition defined perfectly well the range of examples in mind initially (such as squares, rectangles, parallelograms). Criticism 3 draws attention to a visual interpretation of that definition that allows properties not originally intended. Indeed, the definition is rejected, and an additional constraint is added to achieve definition 3. A similar phenomenon occurs in the transition from definition 3 to definition 4.

The decisions to accept the criticisms are not really about what is a priori true about quadrilaterals (or finding the "real" definition), but instead are about context and values, as we discussed in relation to Essential Understanding 3*a*. More specifically, the prelude to definition 3 points to the ways in which a definition can be subordinated to a theorem. One might have a theorem that works for a certain class of objects, and when a counterexample is proposed that unsettles the theorem, one can change the definition of the

→ Essential
Understanding 3*a*

Geometric objects can have different definitions. Some are better than others, and their worth depends both on context and values.

object to rescue the theorem. We discuss the relationship between definitions and theorems more in our elaboration of Big Idea 4.

The prelude to definition 4 is more subtle, in that it refuses to admit an inclusive hierarchy of polygons—because that would imply that theorems about triangles should apply to (some) quadrilaterals. In contrast, because concavity did not threaten the theorem in question (sum of the angles), criticism 5 was rejected. However, as we will see later, in case study 3, there may well be desired theorems about quadrilaterals that are menaced by definition 4.

In our discussion of angles, we note that all the definitions that we considered admitted the straight angle (which can seem a little oxymoronic) as a bona fide angle. However, in definition 4, this type of angle is excluded when the property of collinearity is rejected. We thus see how closely connected, but also contingent, definitions are. Indeed, the great geometer H. S. M. Coxeter (1987, pp. 5–6) compared geometric definitions to dictionary entries: when you look up one word, you find in its definition another word that needs to be looked up, which gives a definition of still another word, and so on, *without a real starting point on which all definitions depend.*

Big Idea 4

A written proof is the endpoint of the process of proving.

On Process and Proof in Geometry: Big Idea 4

Developing Essential Understanding of Proof and Proving for Teaching Mathematics in Grades 9–12 (Ellis, Bieda, and Knuth, forthcoming) contains a full discussion of different types of proofs and the process of proving, including the development of conjectures and arguments with examples from different areas of mathematics.

Big Idea 4. *A written proof is the endpoint of the process of proving.*

Writing a formal proof of a geometric result is the endpoint of a significant piece of mathematical investigation. It is not generally an activity to be undertaken on its own. In particular, it occurs *after* an invariance has been detected, conjectured, and tested against a context of variation; *after* an appropriate diagram has been constructed and understood; and *after* relevant definitions have been brought into play. All of these are components of the process of proving. They also connect to the three big ideas previously discussed in this book, and they all come together in attempts to compose formal, deductive proofs.

Different proofs provide a varied balance between showing *that* something must always be the case (and could not have been otherwise, or, contrariwise, could never happen, no matter how hard one tried) and showing *why* something is necessarily so. This latter aspect refers to illumination, which some proofs provide more than others. This clarity or insight usually arises from the familiarity of the prover with the situation—from things that he or she initially noticed tacitly, before realizing their significance more explicitly in the course of investigation and finally bringing them to bear in a conventionally linear and deductive account. But first, how can a conjecture be tested?

Testing conjectures

Essential Understanding 4a. *Empirical verification is an important part of the process of proving, but it can never, by itself, constitute a proof.*

A conjecture is a proposition that has not yet been proved or disproved. In school geometry, the conjectures are, on the whole, already there. This is unfortunate, since students are then not even remotely engaged in the whole proving process, in which the making of conjectures can be the most creative and motivating part. As a consequence, students experience the activity of "doing proofs" without opportunities for curiosity and inquiry. The broader activity of proof construction involves a marshalling and systematizing of experience, insight, reasons, constructions, and arguments, gained through an exploration of a specific situation—often over an appreciable period of time. In this book, we try to offer you opportunities to make and test your own geometric conjectures.

When trying to prove something, you need to have the conjecture already and to have tested it to the best of your ability, including examining specific instances. Such an approach is often called *inductive*. At its most basic, it is an argument based on very limited evidence. We hear this kind of argument when a student says, "It worked for a few different triangles, so it works." Balacheff (1988, p. 218) calls this practice, which involves a claim of proof on the basis of a slim weight of evidence, "naïve empiricism."

As proof practice gains sophistication, it can move to what Balacheff (following Francis Bacon) calls the "crucial experiment," which involves checking the conjecture against an instance of the conjecture that has not yet been checked and asserting that "if it works here it will always work" (p. 219). For example, after you test your initial conjecture and find that it works for a few prototypical triangles, you check it on a specific scalene triangle to see if it still works. If it does, then you might move on to offering a proof by *generic example*, where you use mathematical properties and structure on a generic case (so it is still on a specific instance, but the argument is oriented towards the general) to explain why the conjecture must always be true. One of the reasons why we devoted so much of the discussion of Big Idea 2 to variance and invariance is that we believe that students are less likely to mistake an argument based on naïve expericism for an argument based on a crucial experiment if they have a sense of the infinite variability of almost any geometric situation.

An inductive exploration begins with simply generating experience and information and is the likely source of the conjecture. When faced with subsequent "particular cases," the examining eye shifts as awareness dawns: these cases are not simply more of the same isolated instances. The eye has a history now of looking at these situations in order. The examining eye is interested not just in confirming the *what* for yet another instance; it also becomes interested in thinking about the *why*. The observer starts to look at the next specific situation with an eye not only on the emerging pattern but also on the objects and relationships that may be causally involved in creating or being responsible for the invariance—and this sets the stage for the proof by generic example.

Consider your earlier work with Reflect 1.9 and our ensuing discussion as an illustration of this stage-setting process. In Reflect 1.9, you saw that the midpoint triangle is always a triangle similar to the starting triangle. One of the what-if-not? suggestions that we subsequently made was to consider joining midpoints of quadrilaterals to create other quadrilaterals. As a consequence, we already have gone through the first stages of exploring invariance and variance. Reflect 1.17 invites you to take the next step with respect to some of these conjectures.

Big Idea 2

Geometry is about working with variance and invariance, despite appearing to be about theorems.

Reflect 1.17

What would be involved in moving toward proving the conjectures that the midpoints of a quadrilateral always form a parallelogram?

Try a range of different types of starting quadrilaterals. Does the tentative generalization about the new quadrilateral being at least as special as the old hold? Why or why not?

Before trying to prove this conjecture, you might want to start with some examples. Often starting with simple examples—in this case, a square or a rectangle—can help to provide a sense of how the relationships are working. Then you might try an arbitrary triangle to confirm, perhaps just visually, or perhaps by measuring, that the conjecture does indeed hold. Using a DGE, you might begin with an arbitrary quadrilateral and then drag it into more specific configurations (such as a square or rectangle) in order to look for patterns. You want to be sure the conjecture holds empirically. Mathematician George Pólya (1954/1990), ventriloquizing in the character of a traditional mathematics professor, advises us to wait before starting to prove a statement:

> If you have to prove a theorem, do not rush. First of all, understand fully what the theorem says, try to see clearly what it means. Then check the theorem; it could be false. Examine the consequences, verify as many particular instances as are needed to convince yourself of the truth. When you have satisfied yourself that the theorem is true, you start proving it. (p. 76)

The different possibilities for testing will also inform your attempts at generating a proof. Although DGEs offer only empirical evidence about a conjecture, the number of cases that can be considered is incomparably larger than it would be with only paper-and-pencil constructions. In addition, DGEs provide both an important sense of continuity in the experience of dragging and the consequent visual feedback on the screen. The continuous motion on the screen blurs the discreteness of individual examples but can seem compelling when aspects of the situation remain unchanged. In this case, by dragging the vertices of your initial quadrilateral, you will see that the opposite sides of the midpoint quadrilateral remain parallel.

Look back at the origin of the conjecture as you attempt to prove it: what are the things that are changing beneath the invariance? In addition to the opposite sides remaining parallel, they also remain the same length. If you continue in the domain of parallelograms, rectangles and squares, you will also notice that the four triangles formed around the midpoint quadrilateral almost remain invariant. This might offer a good starting point for a proof. Identifying these invariances will help you attend to the salient features of the situation that the proof *must* ultimately engage with and help you to comprehend. When looking at variation, it is also a good time to look for counterexamples and perhaps refine your conjecture.

What to do with a counterexample

Essential Understanding 4b. *Counterexamples are important: individual instances can disprove a conjecture, but they can also lead to modified conjectures.*

Although a counterexample is sufficient to disprove a conjecture, and although an example is not sufficient to prove a claim about what is true of a larger set of objects, a counterexample to a conjecture is not necessarily a mathematical full stop or a signal to dismiss the conjecture completely. There may be a way to work around the counterexample—particularly if it really is just one or even a few isolated cases that are problematic.

Imre Lakatos (1976), in his book *Proofs and Refutations*, proposes a colorful terminology for different ways of responding to the presence of counterexamples, which he, on historical grounds, terms "monsters." He describes two central ways to deal with counterexamples. One way, "monster-barring," involves finding a way to exclude the problematic example, sometimes by means of a retreat to safety by radically restricting the domain of applicability of the conjecture. The other way, "monster-adjustment," involves finding a different way of seeing the particular counterexample so that it loses its force as a counterexample: it is explained away. Consider the examples of conjectures in Reflect 1.18.

Reflect 1.18

Decide which of the conjectures below you believe and which ones you think need modifying. For each of the latter, if you were offering a student a counterexample, which one would you provide and why? How might you modify those conjectures in need of modification? Notice in particular *how* you go about this part of the task.

a. The perpendicular bisectors of the sides of a triangle always meet inside the triangle.

b. A triangle always has a longest side.

c. Through any three points you can always draw a circle.

d. Through any four points you can always draw a circle.

e. The diagonals of a quadrilateral always intersect.

Although Reflect 1.18 can be seen as work with counterexamples in relation to revising conjectures, it also provides good practice in being precise about the scope and limitations of geometric claims. Notice that none of the revisions mentioned in the following paragraphs does anything toward actively proving the claim.

Comments on conjecture (a)

Offer an obtuse triangle. A monster-barring reaction is to exclude the whole category (and perhaps right triangles too—what does *inside* mean?). So revise the conjecture by adding the word *acute* before *triangle*. Notice that this might be too large a retreat. Are there *any* right or obtuse-angled triangles for which the conjecture is nevertheless true?

Comments on conjecture (b)

Offer an isosceles triangle. In such a case, there might not be a unique longest side. Offer an equilateral triangle. There would not be a longest at all, since here all three sides have the same length. A monster-barring move is to revise the statement by adding the word *scalene* before *triangle*.

Comments on conjecture (c)

Offer three collinear points. No plane circle can go through three collinear points (unless a straight line is counted as a circle of infinite radius). Revise the statement by adding *non-collinear* in front of *points*. Notice that these three points determine a triangle. Another way of stating the conjecture is that any triangle can have a circle drawn through its vertices (thus, the conjecture alternatively claims that every triangle is *cyclic*). This circle is called the *circumcircle* of the triangle. What is needed to draw a circle, called the *incircle*, *inside* a given triangle?

Comments on conjecture (d)

Result (c) says (does it?) that there is a unique circle through three points. If we pick a fourth point not on that circle, there cannot be a circle through all four points. But such circles do exist on occasion—for example, if the four points are the corners of a square or a rectangle (where is the center of the circumcircle?). So what is the set of quadrilaterals (known as cyclic quadrilaterals) for which this result is true? Are they an already-named family (such as kites or rhombuses)? What property or properties characterizes them, and why? No revision to this conjecture is obvious, so more exploration is needed.

There is a common characterization of a property of cyclic quadrilaterals (involving their opposite angles); because this is an "if and only if" result, it could also be used as a defining property for the class. However, the class of cyclic quadrilaterals does not interact with any other type of quadrilateral (other than squares or rectangles, both of which lie inside it), in that there are both in-stances and non-instances of every other named type that are cyclic. Cyclic quadrilaterals have an angle property that is comparable to that of parallelograms: the former have opposite angle sums of two right angles, while the latter have adjacent angles adding to this sum.

Comments on conjecture (e)

Offer the dart (or concave kite). At least two revisions are feasible in the face of this counterexample.

"Monster-adjust" the definition of diagonal to require that it cannot lie outside the figure (does the figure always have a clearly defined "inside"?), thereby endeavoring to pull the monster's teeth. Notice that in so doing, you do not change the scope of the original claim, as in the previous four instances. A different move is to re-strict the conjecture to convex quadrilaterals. Acknowledge that the original conjecture as made is incorrect.

If you fiddle with a definition, it will no longer be clear in the statement of the theorem that the monstrous situation raised by the dart has been handled. Also, if the dart were the only counterex-ample, then it could simply be monster-barred by saying, "The di-agonals of any quadrilateral (except the dart) always meet." But it is rare to have singular or isolated counterexamples in geometry.

Argumentation and proof

In the mathematics education literature, the term *argumentation* ap-plies to the various rhetorical means that can be used to convince someone else of the truth or falsity of a claim. Whenever students are discussing the truth or falsity of claims in mathematics class, you have instances of argumentation. Some students will try to argue by empirical means or on empirical grounds ("It worked in these cases"), some might try convincing on aesthetic grounds ("It's got to be right," "It's so clear," or, "It's so simple"), and some might try "convincing by intimidation" (shouting down or gesticulating wildly to try to convince another of their position).

There is a language of argumentation that partially overlaps that of proof: argumentation includes use of the words *because* and *so* to signal links between previous and subsequent utterances. *Because* indicates an offering of reasons *why* something happens, while the construction "when..., then..." records a noticing of some-thing about a relationship. Verb phrases like "must be," "has to be," "has got to be," or "cannot be" get used, as does the interesting con-necting phrase "which means that" (we use it ourselves, below).

In more formal mathematical proof, words like *hence*, *since*, and *therefore*, and "if..., then..." constructions are widely used. You might record yourself talking your way through a proof of something to someone and see which words you tend to use, in which circumstances you use them, and whether you possibly use them with differing intents.

French mathematics educator Nicolas Balacheff (1999) has offered a nice analogy to capture the relationship of argumentation to proof:

argumentation : a conjecture :: mathematical proof : a theorem

One difference between argumentation and proof is that argumentation is always about the content, whereas proof is sometimes about questions of the form or nature of an argument more generally. Part of a proof is its acceptability with regard to the *form* of the argument, irrespective of the content. Tasks that begin, "Prove that...," are often less likely to produce argumentation than tasks that additionally require the production of a conjecture. It is from argumentation that the origin of a proof often arises. In what follows, we will offer several examples of both argumentation and proof.

What's the idea?

Essential Understanding 4c. *Behind every proof is a proof idea.*

The genesis of a proof is one of the hardest things to speak or write about, particularly in generalities. Most geometric proofs contain a single central proof idea. Too often, students, and even teachers, think, "I just have to remember the right steps, in the right order." It can become an issue of memory, almost like reciting a poem. In particular, the two-column proof format obscures the proof idea—the central realization that drives a proof and makes it cohere as more than a series of statements, one after the other. As an example, consider the specifics requiring further justification in Reflect 1.19.

Reflect 1.19

The sequence of diagrams from left to right in figure 1.31 represents the essence of a transformation-based proof of a well-worn result about the area of a triangle. See if you can identify the proof idea and document what specifics still need proving.

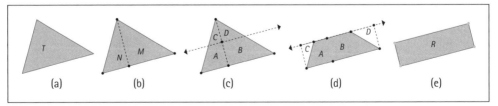

Fig. 1.31. What is going on?

The sequence of pictures in figure 1.31 suggests a number of claims that need verifying. We need to justify that the resulting figure in the last diagram *is* a rectangle—in other words, that what looks right *is* right. But the proof idea contains the essence of the argument and provides insight into *why* the area of a triangle is, in this formulation, *base times half-height*. More specifically, why do *C* and *D* come together to make a straight line (notice that this claim is tacitly made by means of the notation of the fourth image in the figure), how is the dotted line chosen that creates *M* and *N*, and what is its relationship to the base? Can any triangle be dealt with in the same manner? And so on. But the central proof idea involving a specific decomposition and rearrangement of a triangle is clear and, to us, compelling. Reflect 1.20 considers the proof ideas behind familiar theorems.

Reflect 1.20

Select a couple of theorems from your school's geometry curriculum, and ask, "What is the proof idea?"

Consider, for example, if you did not do so in Reflect 1.20, the proof of the conjecture about the midpoint triangle being congruent to the other three "inside" triangles in Reflect 1.9 (the triangles labeled *M*, *A*, *B*, and *C* in fig. 1.32). Given that we want to prove a congruence result, we might try to show whether the sides and angles of *M* are congruent to the corresponding parts of *A*, *B*, and *C*. What strategy might we use? If we know Thales's theorem, we might try to apply it: it guarantees that segments *HI* and *GF* will be parallel, since *H* and *I* are both midpoints of segments *GE* and *EF*, respectively. Knowing that segments *HI* and *GF* are parallel might help us see several possible transversal lines (*GE*, *HJ*, *JI* and *EF*), which will produce a host of relevant relationships between the angles of our two triangles. So, for example, we know that angle *JHI* is congruent to angle *HJG*.

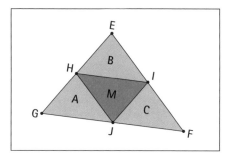

Fig. 1.32. Decomposing a triangle into congruent sub-triangles

This general approach will enable us to make deductions about angles but will not help us explain why the sides of the two triangles should be congruent. We do know that the triangles share side *HJ*. And if we look at the triangle "on its side," we can see another application of Thales's theorem, telling us that segments *IJ* and *EG* are parallel. That means that the quadrilateral *GHIJ* is a parallelogram, which in turn means that *GH* = *IJ* and *HI* = *GJ*. Now we have the main pieces that we need to proceed.

A different proof idea would be to focus right away on the quadrilateral *GHIJ* and show that it is a parallelogram, a fact that directly provides the side-side-side result for triangles *A* and *M*. And we could do the same thing with triangles *M* and *C*, as well as with *M* and *B*. We have not written out the formal proof, but we have a good idea of how to proceed.

Attending to symmetry can help develop very compelling proof ideas. Consider the well-known theorem that an angle subtended by a diameter of a circle is always right (see fig. 1.33). One proof idea (which does not involve symmetry) is to split the angle of interest into two parts, using the fact that the center point (*O*) gives us knowledge about different lengths—so we are turning one triangle into two related ones (see fig. 1.34), which we know much more about, as many sides are radii, including the one splitting the angle of interest into two parts.

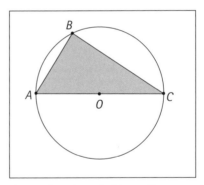

Fig. 1.33. An angle subtended by a diameter of a circle

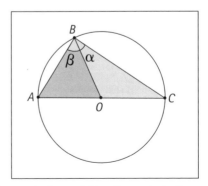

Fig. 1.34. A proof idea for a circle theorem

To elaborate this proof idea, we begin by finding the center of the circle, O, drawing in the radius OB, and showing that the two angles at B form a right angle, based on the fact that triangles ABO and OBC are both isosceles. (Notice how a proof idea relates to and can serve to motivate or even explain particular geometric constructions.) Using the fact that the sum of the angles of triangle ABC is equal to two right angles, the fact that the angle at A is equal to β and that the angle at C is equal to α leads to the desired conclusion that $\beta + \alpha$ is a right angle. Reflect 1.21 provides an opportunity to develop an alternative proof idea.

Reflect 1.21

Try to develop an alternative proof idea—one that uses symmetry to construct an argument about an angle subtended by a diameter of a circle.

A different proof idea that draws on a symmetry argument might begin by using the diameter as a line of reflectional symmetry—that line seems perfect for reflection, since it is also a line of reflectional symmetry for the circle. Once the reflection is constructed, a new shape appears—namely, a quadrilateral that looks like a kite (see fig. 1.35). We can convince ourselves that it is in fact a kite by considering the way in which it was constructed, but what is more important is that B', the reflection of B, falls on the circle—thanks to the symmetry of the circle. That fact is important because it means that the kite is also a cyclic quadrilateral, and that means that its opposite angles are supplementary. That, in turn, means that both angle ABC and angle $AB'C$ are right angles (since they are also congruent).

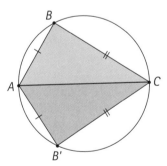

Fig. 1.35. A proof idea involving reflectional symmetry

The proof idea through symmetry draws attention to different aspects of the objects involved. Instead of focusing on isosceles triangles, it gives the kite the central role and invites a link to cyclic quadrilaterals. (What do cyclic quadrilaterals and kites have to do with each other?) You might try a similar approach by using rotation around the center of the circle to obtain a rectangle. Working with different proof ideas can underline the way in which different proofs depend on different assumptions and properties—an awareness that is very important when the time comes to turn the proof idea into a written proof.

Proof and variation

Essential Understanding 4d. Geometry uses a wide variety of kinds of proofs.

Additional discussion of the difference between transformations as processes of change and transformations as objects in their own right appears in *Developing Essential Understanding of Geometry for Teaching Mathematics in Grades 6–8* (Sinclair, Pimm, and Skelin 2012).

Not every proof in geometry fits the conventional two-column deductive proof structure. In our discussion of Essential Understanding 4d, we focus on transformations of the plane, seen as objects in their own right. The middle school curriculum devotes a great deal of attention to these transformations but treats them as processes of change rather than as mathematical objects in their own right (for example, "rotating" rather than "a rotation"). In high school, with the sustained move toward a functions orientation, the mathematical status of geometric transformations alters (we return to this topic in chapter 2).

One of the useful ways of classifying transformations of the plane, especially isometries, comes from looking at the set of points left invariant under the transformation—the task that Reflect 1.22 asks you to undertake.

Reflect 1.22

A theorem asserts that there are only four types of isometries: translations, rotations, reflections, and glide reflections. Examine each one to determine its set of invariant points.

If we view an isometry as a congruence-preserving transformation, and a transformation as a type of function, then what possibilities arise from composing two isometries? This exploration is significantly aided by technology. Suppose that we start with combinations of transformations of the same type. What is the result of the composition of two different reflections?

If two lines of reflection are parallel to one another, it is relatively easy to see: the combined result is a translation by twice the distance between the lines in direction of the perpendicular. We know from this exploration that translations (other than the identity translation, which maps each point to itself) have no invariant points and that reflections have an entire line's worth. However, the invariant points under the first reflection are subsequently moved by the second one, so there are no invariant points under the composition.

If the two lines of reflection are not parallel to each other, then the result is a rotation, as we argue below. One argument arises from looking at the set of invariant points. What stays fixed under this composite transformation? One point does (the point of intersection of the two lines of reflection). What could this composite transformation be?

It is an isometry (because each component transformation is), so our theorem claims that it is one of the four types on the list. It cannot be a non-identity translation or a glide reflection (they have no fixed points). And it cannot be a reflection—otherwise, where is the invariant line? Furthermore, it exhibits no change in handedness (orientation). So it must be a rotation, and the sole fixed point is the center of rotation of the transformation that is the composition. The angle of rotation is twice the angle between the two lines (the angle from the first to the second lines of reflection).

We have been discussing the three isometries of translation, rotation, and reflection and their underlying motions (translating, rotating, and reflecting). The fourth isometry that might be encountered in school geometry is the glide reflection. Given that this isometry can be seen as a combination (in either order) of a reflection and a translation along the line of reflection, many students wonder why it is given the same status as the other three (or why does it not have a single-word name). In fact, the fourth is included as a matter of closure when considering two particular features of isometries: whether or not they have fixed points—points that do not move under the isometry but are invariant while all around them are changing—and whether or not they preserve handedness.

A non-identity translation has no fixed points, nor does a glide reflection. Rotations and reflections both have fixed points (a non-identity rotation has a single fixed point, and a reflection has an entire fixed line of such points). Reflections and glide reflections change handedness, but rotations and translations do not. A glide reflection is an isometry that complements the other three. Neither preserving handedness nor having any fixed points, it fills the fourth space in the 2 × 2 table shown in figure 1. 36.

Any fixed points?		Preserves handedness?	
		Yes	No
	Yes	Rotation	Reflection
	No	Translation	Glide reflection

Fig. 1.36. A broad classification of isometries
by invariants

We have said little yet about one final interesting isometry—namely, the identity transformation, which does nothing to anything since it leaves every single point in the plane fixed. You might say this is not much of a transformation. Nevertheless, this transformation is an isometry for which every point is a fixed point. Every point is consequently invariant! It also preserves orientation. How do we fit this into what we have said about isometries?

First, what sort of isometry is it? We could see it as a zero-rotation or as a zero-translation—we could not find a way to see it as a reflection or a glide reflection. But its fixed-point set is not the same as the set that we claimed for either rotations (one) or translations (none). Instead, it is a whole plane's worth of fixed points. Our preference is to see it is a zero-rotation about the origin. In chapter 2, where we explore matrix specifications of certain isometries, we will see that, presuming this identity transformation to be a rotation about the origin, a very simple matrix similar to those used for rotations works for it. So, one way of resolving the question of whether the identity transformation is a rotation or a translation is to insist that a translation, by definition, involves shifting every point a *non-zero* distance in a given direction, while allowing a zero angle of rotation.

What is the composition of two rotations? We begin with two proposed arguments.

> **Proposed argument 1:** Seemingly, the composition of two rotations must be a translation if the centers of rotation are not identical, because the one single point invariant under the first rotation is not invariant under the second.

> **Response: Argument 2:** No, it is not a translation. Why? Because a DGE shows that it is not (see fig. 1.37). It is a rotation (if C_1 is the center of rotation taking A to A' and C_2 is the center of rotation taking A' to A'', then C_3 is the center of rotation taking A to A''). But why? And where is the center of rotation in relation to the ones that we start with? And what will be the composite angle of rotation?

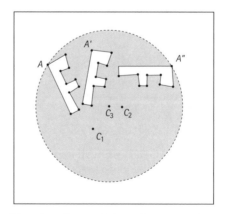

Fig. 1.37. Composition of two rotations

Surprise can provide an excellent motivation for proof here. We found a counterexample to our conjecture, so we must refute it. Further, we have good evidence that the composition of two rotations is a rotation. But perhaps there are counterexamples to this, too.

A geometric investigation and the question of proof

Essential
Understanding 3*b*

We now present case study 3, this chapter's final case study, whose purpose is to indicate ways in which the activities of varying, conjecturing, diagramming, defining, and proving are codependent. We have already discussed the codependence of defining and conjecturing, in the sense that definitions can change in response to the desire to preserve certain theorems or to produce statements of theorems that are as simple as possible. We also drew attention in our discussion of Essential Understanding 3*b* to the way in which defining and classifying relate.

Definitions in geometry are of two distinct types: definition by genesis (how you can create the object) and definition by property (how you can characterize the object in terms of certain features).

Case Study 3: Diagonals of polygons

Revisiting an earlier theme of needing to know what counts as a thing in order to be able to count things correctly, carry out the task in Reflect 1.23 before reading on.

> ### Reflect 1.23
>
> If a polygon has *n* sides, how many diagonals can (does? must?) it have? Come up with a conjecture, test it in a variety of ways, and attempt to prove your result.

A standard way of approaching this task is to begin empirically with a set of exemplar polygons with different numbers of sides and then draw in their diagonals to be able to count them (see fig. 1.38). (Secondary school student work related to this problem can be found in Balacheff [1988].) You might well have noticed that the number of diagonals does not seem to change for a polygon with a fixed number of sides, and you also might have started to think about *why* it might be so. What determines a diagonal?

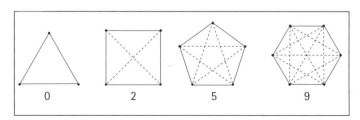

0   2   5   9

Fig. 1.38. Diagonals of regular polygons

The observation that every polygon with the same fixed number of sides has the same number of diagonals can lead to a conjecture related to the number of diagonals that should be added as the number of sides increase. For example, the number of diagonals in a heptagon is five more than for the hexagon, and is therefore 14. We can check this fact for a few more sequences of polygons and make a conjecture. But the conjecture may seem weak, in that it does not immediately predict the number of diagonals inside an n-sided polygon. We could undertake some algebraic work to come up with a closed formula, working just with the numbers. However, to understand *why* this formula works, we must do more work with the diagonals themselves.

Diagonals cannot be formed between a given vertex and the two adjacent ones (why?). Because the quadrilateral, for example, has only four sides, it will have just one diagonal coming from every vertex. The pentagon will have two (5 take away 3) from each of its five vertices, and, in general, $n - 3$ diagonals will come from each of n vertices. Thus, there are $n(n - 3)$ diagonals leaving the vertices. The main proof idea is here: isolate one vertex and look at what happens there, because every vertex is alike in this respect. We then just need to scale up our analysis, by multiplying by the number of vertices.

But $n(n - 3)$ is too many diagonals. We have over-counted. Because every diagonal joins two vertices, we have counted each one exactly twice (for instance, once going from A to B and once going from B to A). Consequently, there are only $n(n - 3)/2$ diagonals in total. The effort to try to understand how the number of diagonals relates to the polygon effectively shapes our understanding of diagonals in a polygon. It does so by elaborating on the symmetry of the situation in terms of the number of diagonals emerging from each vertex (ignoring the particularities of the location of the vertex and stressing what it has in common with every other vertex), as well as by the restrictions that they must subscribe to, including the fact that they all pass inside the polygon.

This conjecture and proof idea could now be written up as a *theorem* about polygons and their diagonals: that is, as a statement, together with a proof, as requested in Reflect 1.24.

Reflect 1.24

Reflecting on the preceding exploration of polygons and their diagonals, write a statement and proof, the combination of which constitutes a theorem. Then record the main proof idea—the main "vision" that constitutes this theorem—and the main diagram that relates to it.

Although experimenting with dragging polygons in a DGE might reinforce this argument, it might also serve to challenge or undermine it. Additionally, it can throw into sharp relief certain beliefs about diagonals and how they might be erroneous. Reflect 1.25 asks you to explore the possibilities in a DGE.

Reflect 1.25

Create a quadrilateral, a pentagon, a hexagon, and a heptagon in a DGE. Draw in the diagonals. Change the shape of the specific polygons by dragging a single vertex. What do you notice? In particular, do diagonals ever seem to disappear or crop up in unexpected places?

Yes, diagonals do seem to vanish or appear unexpectedly. One diagonal seemingly disappears each time three vertices of the polygon become collinear, and furthermore, some of the lines being counted as "diagonals" occur in unexpected places (e.g., completely outside the figure when the vertex "goes" concave, or actually lying "along" or "on top of" sides of the polygon itself).

Now consider the four polygons shown in figure 1.39 (a quadrilateral, a pentagon, a hexagon, and a heptagon) in relation to the original conjecture and purported proof. One might want to say that the quadrilateral shown has one diagonal, thereby providing a counterexample to the theorem. Where do you think the problem lies? Is it with the theorem itself? If so, what was wrong with the proof? Or perhaps the difficulty might lead us to a reconsideration of the definition of a diagonal (which you may not have even considered: definitions are often taken for granted and assumed to be shared until counterexamples start cropping up). Is the definition perhaps too broad if it allows as diagonals those lines that fall outside the figure (or along it, quite literally as borderline cases)?

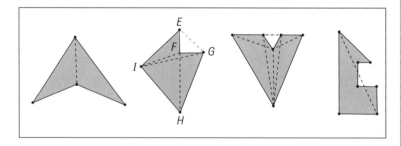

Fig. 1.39. Various polygons and some of their diagonals

There are at least two ways to rescue the theorem: (1) restrict its domain by saying that the number of diagonals in a *convex* polygon is $n(n - 3)/2$ and saying nothing about what happens in the case of non-convex polygons; or (2) acknowledge that the definition of diagonal includes lines that may pass outside the polygon, in which case the number of diagonals in the concave quadrilateral is indeed two—one just happens to lie inside and one outside.

In the second figure, not only do we have "diagonals" outside the polygon *HIEFG*, but also, if every vertex is joined to each of the other vertices that are not adjacent, we have only four diagonals, since the segment from *E* to *H* necessarily passes through the vertex adjacent to *E*—namely, *F*—and there should be five, according to the theorem. Once again, if we want to save the theorem, we would need to restrict the definition of diagonal from the inclusive one (perhaps of a line segment joining any two distinct nonadjacent vertices of the polygon). In the process, we change the domain of applicability of the theorem without changing the nature of the claim itself.

Alternately, we could change the domain of the theorem to state that no three of the vertices of the polygon can be collinear. If we take this route, we are free to try to formulate a new conjecture about the number of diagonals in a polygon that contains collinear vertices. Note that the third figure contains four collinear vertices, which may lead to a different conjecture from that for polygons that contain three collinear vertices. Given the complexities that ensue, we might choose to maintain the broad definition of diagonal to retain the one cohesive theorem. But that would mean broadening one's example space of what can arise as a diagonal of a polygon considerably.

Regardless of what we decide to do, the process of conjecturing, which essentially involves the production of examples and counterexamples relative to some claim or generalization, affects the processes of both proving and defining the concepts involved in making the claim. The elaboration of definitions contributes in significant ways to the enrichment of the concept image associated with the notion of a diagonal. And we might need to continue to elaborate the definition of *diagonal*: the fourth figure suggests a new kind of diagonal that lies *both* inside and outside the polygon while not passing through any other vertices of sides. And who knows what other complexities might occur with a seventeen-million-sided polygon, not the least of which might be ascertaining where the "inside" actually is.

A conventional definition of diagonal leads to a straightforward mathematical proof that ignores the wide diversity of polygons to which it is applied (as well as the generic mental image of polygons being convex, and even regular), as well as to an unnecessarily abrupt end to the process of conjecturing. However, a deeper appreciation of some geometric consequences of that definition, in terms of the possibilities for "diagonals," might throw into question why the two sides of a polygon adjacent to any vertex "obviously" do not *count* as diagonals, when other segments that are diagonals may completely cover a side. Perhaps the theorem's formula should be $n(n-1)/2$?

Further, in the process of exploring the diversity of polygons and the range of diagonals, pseudo-diagonals, and non-diagonals, we might very well arrive at an alternate means of classifying polygons. In particular, in addition to the convex/concave distinction that is more familiar, might we not consider polygons with or without collinear vertices or polygons whose diagonals lie both inside and outside the polygon, as subclasses of concave polygons?

Alternative ways of classifying polygons can lead to different definitions of a mathematical concept. A concave polygon, for example, has at least three definitions:

1. **Any polygon that is not convex** (a negative definition, throwing us back on our ability to identify a polygon in general and a convex one more specifically)

2. **Any polygon with at least one interior angle measuring more than 180 degrees** (a definition by property, though seemingly requiring us to examine every single angle in the polygon. How "almost convex" can a polygon be and yet still have at least one reflex angle? Can it have just one such angle?)

3. **Any polygon for which there exists a straight line that cuts it in four or more points** (a definition by property, though giving us no genesis idea about how we might find such a line. Can there be a concave polygon where only one such line exists?)

Reflect 1.26 engages you in an exploration of these three definitions of a concave polygon. Reflect 1.27 asks you to build on images that you develop through the exploration.

Reflect 1.26

Undertake a study of concave polygons and check whether the three definitions above are equivalent; in other words, do all of them identify exactly the same set of polygons as concave?

Be sure to draw figures, and perhaps even start a "zoo" with different types of concave polygons: which ones belong together, and why?

Reflect 1.27

How would you respond to the following attempt to provide an overall direct image for a concave polygon: "Concave polygons look as though they are collapsed or have one or more angles dented in."

Could you provide a similar "gestalt" for convex polygons? How useful do you find such characterizations?

The foregoing case study of the diagonals of a quadrilateral is somewhat analogous to the rich and intricate story that Lakatos (1976) recounts in *Proofs and Refutations*, which documents in a historically sensitive and engaging fashion how complicated the interrelationships among theorems, definitions, and proofs can be. Lakatos presents a detailed case study of the claim (first written about by Descartes) that for all polyhedra, $V - E + F = 2$, where V is the number of vertices, E the number of edges, and F the number of faces of the polyhedron.

For more than a century, attempts to prove or to refute this claim as true for *all* polyhedra plunged eminent mathematicians into what Lakatos has his character *Iota* refer to as "the fundamental dialectical unity of proofs and refutations" (p. 37). Mathematicians proposed many possible definitions, offered and then amended putative proofs, and showered purported examples and counterexamples like confetti on the problem. With the examples and reflections that we have offered in this chapter, we have tried to be true to the spirit of mathematical investigation that Lakatos's writing embodies, albeit in a far more limited and certainly ahistoric way. We strongly recommend Lakatos's book to high school geometry teachers.

Conclusion

The first three big ideas draw attention to the way in which doing geometry involves working with diagrams, looking for variance and invariance, and formulating definitions. The process of proving, as articulated in Big Idea 4, involves elements of all the first three big ideas: making and testing conjectures can lead to formulating new definitions, which may in turn involve generating new diagrams. These diagrams can provide the basis for proof ideas.

In chapter 2, we consider the way in which these big ideas relate across the curriculum to coordinate geometry and trigonometry. We also illustrate how the way of thinking about geometry described in this chapter is useful in examining how, for example, transformations can be a uniting thread from grades 6–8 all the way to college mathematics.

Chapter

2

Connections: Looking Back and Ahead in Learning

As the NCTM (2000) Content Standards for geometry indicate, geometry not only is an area of mathematical study in its own right but also is connected—through the use of imagery and diagrams as well as specific ideas and results—to ideas and problems across mathematics. Big Idea 2, which captures the importance of perceiving and working with invariance across variation, is the primary insight that we draw on in chapter 2, where we look at the development and connections of geometric thinking both *horizontally*, across other areas of mathematics taught in the high school years, and *vertically*, in the years leading up to and beyond grades 9–12.

Big Idea 4, which recognizes written proof as the culmination of the process of arguing and explaining, extends across content strands and grades in important ways that are treated in separate volumes in the Essential Understanding Series. For details on conjecturing, generalizing, and reasoning across mathematical contexts and grade levels, see *Developing Essential Understanding of Proof and Proving for Teaching Mathematics in Grades 9–12* (Ellis, Bieda, and Knuth, forthcoming) and *Developing Essential Understanding of Mathematical Reasoning for Teaching Mathematics in Prekindergarten–Grade 8* (Lannin, Ellis, and Elliott 2011).

Thinking through invariance can involve reframing questions and ways of looking at situations to highlight what is changing and what is staying the same despite other things changing. Although algebraic work employs the notion of variable (often designated by x) to allow working on all instances of something at the same time, geometry has no corresponding symbol. Even though geometers work on whole classes of figures at the same time (e.g., all right triangles, all rectangles with a given perimeter, all angles subtended by the diameter of a circle) and rarely, if ever, work only on a particular figure or configuration, the static geometric diagram is not a counterpart to the algebraic x.

Big Idea 2

Geometry is about working with variance and invariance, despite appearing to be about theorems.

Big Idea 4

A written proof is the endpoint of the process of proving.

In algebra, variables such as *x* take on many meanings— for details, see *Developing Essential Understanding of Equations, Expressions, and Functions for Teaching Mathematics in Grades 6–8* (Lloyd, Herbel-Eisenmann, and Star 2011).

DGEs make apparent the specificity and particularity of a single instance of a configuration by allowing its deformation into another like one at the touch of a mouse. Dragging emphasizes the continuity of figures within families subject to the same constraints, such as that *this* point must always lie on *that* line, and the center of *this* circle must always fall on *that* perimeter.

Looking Horizontally at High School Mathematics

In keeping with our approach in chapter 1, we have opted to indicate connections that extend across high school mathematics by means of two case studies: the case of coordinate geometry and the case of trigonometry.

Coordinate geometry

Measurement as attention to attributes of objects is discussed in *Developing Essential Understanding of Number and Numeration for Teaching Mathematics in Prekindergarten– Grade 2* (Dougherty et al. 2010).

We have chosen to include coordinate geometry as a horizontal *extension* in high school geometry, even though it is often taken as an integral part of the geometry strand (as in the NCTM Standards [2000]). We have done so because coordinate geometry provides, in essence, an algebraic way of working with geometric shapes. In this sense, coordinate geometry is not dissimilar to measurement, which assigns numbers based on units to attributes of a geometric object and involves formulas for relating these numbers to, say, an object's area or perimeter. Coordinate geometry marks every point in the plane by an (x, y) coordinate pair and, through this assignment, enables us to work numerically and algebraically with segments (e.g., using the distance formula) and angles (e.g., using the slopes of lines to determine whether they form a right angle).

A major use of the coordinate system in the high school geometry curriculum is in the representation of transformations. For example, it turns the geometric fact that a point and its image, when reflected across the y-axis, are equidistant to the line of reflection into the algebraic fact that the coordinates of the reflected image of a point (x, y) is $(-x, y)$. For special cases, the switch provides nice results, though for others (e.g., rotation around a point that is not the origin), the relationship between the coordinates of a point and its image is far less informative. The use of coordinate geometry to work with transformations can provide a good background for working with matrices in the context of linear transformations, since matrices offer yet another way of representing certain transformations of the plane—a topic that we discuss later in this chapter.

The historical motivation for the coordinate system was to channel the computational power of algebra into geometric problems. A geometric idea could be transformed into algebraic terms that would be easier to work with, and then the result could be brought back to bear on the geometric configuration. Consider the set of questions that we posed in chapter 1 about the intersection of a line with a circle. It seemed visually apparent that this could happen only twice, once, or not at all. But how might we prove this? One way would be to transfer these objects (the line and the circle) into the algebraic frame of systems of linear and quadratic equations in x and y whose solution sets lie in the coordinate plane. To find the common solutions, we can set two expressions for y equal to each other and solve for x. Given that we always obtain a quadratic equation (if we believe the algebra), we can show that there are, indeed, no real number solutions, one, or two. Taking this computation back to the geometric situation, we can now say something about the line and the circle in general. It would be a loss to treat coordinate geometry as a way of moving *away from* geometry, when it can be so useful in working *with* geometry as well.

Trigonometry

One setting in which triangle similarity is very significant is in the definition of the six initial trigonometric functions: sine, cosine, tangent, cotangent, secant, and cosecant. The very word *trigonometry* suggests the "-metry" (measurement) of "trigons" ("three-angles"), a plausible name for triangles and one that is more consistent with the common naming scheme for most other plane shapes.

Sine and cosine of a given angle are usually specified first, in terms of ratios of side lengths of a right triangle containing the particular angle. So, if the angle is itself the starting place (see fig. 2.1), an infinite number of right triangles contain the desired angle. Why does it not matter which one we use?

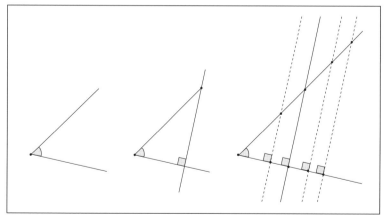

Fig. 2.1. An angle and an associated family of right triangles

Because these triangles are all similar, one to another, the ratios of corresponding sides are always the same. Because all six of

Additional
discussion of
trigonometric
functions and their
applications appears
in *Developing
Essential
Understanding of
Functions
for Teaching
Mathematics in
Grades 9–12* (Cooney,
Beckmann, and Lloyd
2010).

the trigonometric functions are defined as side-length ratios, it does not matter which right triangle we use. So the whole of trigonometry rests on similar triangles and their properties.

An alternative name for the family of trigonometric functions is the *circular functions*, because deriving them from circles is relatively straightforward. There is an important right triangle that is related to the circle as shown in figure 2.2, and it explains where two of the six triangular functions' names come from. The Latin verb *tango* (from which the Argentinian dance derives its name) means "I touch," and a tangent is a "touch-line" of the circle—the term that Robert Record proposed. As mentioned earlier, the Latin verb *seco* means "I cut" (and is the source of the name of the scissor-like gardening tool *secateurs*, as well as the geometric term *sector*—the region of a circle cut off by a *secant* line). So a secant is a "cut-line" of the circle. If θ names the angle in the right triangle at the center of the circle, *and if the radius of the circle is 1 unit*, then the length of the segment shown in color on the tangent line in figure 2.2 is $\tan(\theta)$, and the distance along the secant line from the center of the circle to the tangent line is $\sec(\theta)$ (see the dashed segment shown in color in the figure). Notice that these are definitions by genesis.

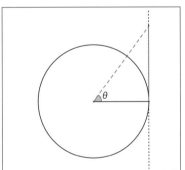

Fig. 2.2. The right triangle that defines the secant and the tangent, using a circle of radius 1

Inside any circle sits a second right triangle that is similar to the first one, as shown in figure 2.3a. This second triangle is more commonly drawn in textbooks and is often displayed without the circle from which it was generated, as in fig. 2.3c. Applying Pythagoras's theorem to each of these two triangles in turn (for the same reason, if the radius is chosen to be 1 unit, $\sin(\theta)$ and $\cos(\theta)$ are the lengths of the two non-radial sides of the smaller triangle) produces two of the common trigonometric identities:

$$1 + [\tan(\theta)]^2 = [\sec(\theta)]^2 \quad \text{and} \quad [\cos(\theta)]^2 + [\sin(\theta)]^2 = 1$$

Being familiar with similar triangles—and the length ratio properties that are invariant across them—is fundamental to high school trigonometry.

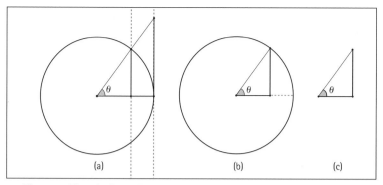

Fig. 2.3. The similar triangles that give rise to the trigonometric definitions

Combining the two perspectives discussed briefly in this section, the unit circle centered at the origin gives $(\cos(\theta), \sin(\theta))$ as the coordinates of one vertex of the smaller right triangle in figure 2.3a and $(1, \tan(\theta))$ as the coordinates of the vertex of the larger right triangle in figure 2.3a. Using similar triangles, it is possible to derive the more common initial definition of $\tan(\theta)$ as the ratio of $\sin(\theta)$ to $\cos(\theta)$ *as a theorem*. Or alternatively, this argument shows the equivalence of the two definitions of $\tan(\theta)$: (1) the length of the segment of the tangent line that goes from the point of tangency (of the unit circle and the tangent line) to the intersection of the other secant line with the tangent line, and (2) the ratio of $\sin(\theta)$ to $\cos(\theta)$.

Looking Vertically at School Geometry

We use a different case—that of transformations in grades 6–8 and in postsecondary mathematics—to illustrate the "vertical" development of geometric thinking in mathematics.

Transformations in grades 6–8

The middle school geometry curriculum, as articulated in NCTM's (2000) Content Standards, provides opportunities for students to work with transformations. Students in grades 6–8 often describe their work colloquially, using terms such as "flips," "turns," "slides," and "zooming." They describe the new sizes, orientations, and positions of shapes under these transformations. Such descriptions are, for the most part, qualitative, and they remain in the visual register. In other words, students in the middle grades work with the fact that a "turn" does not change the orientation of a shape or its size by using a purely visual apprehension of the shape. If asked to identify the transformation linking one shape to its image, students draw on visual strategies. For example, given a shape and its rotated image, as in figure 2.4, students can *see* that one shape is the rotated image of the other, and they may be able to explain some of the reasons for this: the shapes are congruent, and the orientation has not changed. But these are property-based arguments and not definition-based ones.

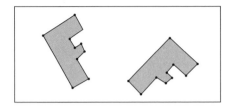

Fig. 2.4. A shape and its rotated image

Furthermore, given a shape, students may be able to sketch its reflected or rotated image. But this can be difficult, since it involves working very closely with the properties of the given transformation. This is particularly true for non-canonical configurations. So, for example, students are likely to find drawing the reflected image in figure 2.5a much easier then doing so in figure 2.5b, since they can use visual approximation to do the former task, but the latter requires them to give more attention to the properties of reflection (unless they turn the piece of paper around, making the line of reflection vertical!).

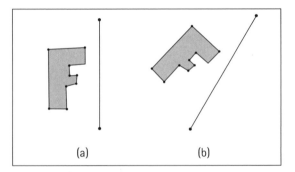

Fig. 2.5. Reflecting a shape across a line of reflection

Similarly, students might be able to identify a line of reflectional symmetry that a shape such as a rectangle or a heart has, but they will probably find it much more challenging to construct, say, the center and angle of rotation in figure 2.4 or the line of reflection in figure 2.6 (especially since it is oblique).

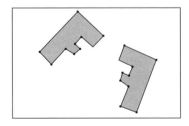

Fig. 2.6. An oblique line of reflection

Constructing the line of reflection involves working backward from the properties—that is, going from the fact that a point and its image have to be equidistant to a line to the idea that the line will therefore pass through the midpoint of the segment connecting the point and its image. Reflect 2.1 challenges you to identify the center of rotation in figure 2.4.

Reflect 2.1

Specifying the particular rotation shown in figure 2.4 requires identifying both the center of rotation and the angle of rotation. Try estimating each first. Which one is easier to identify? What properties of rotation are you using when you identify each one?

You might begin by recognizing that any point on the pre-image shape and its corresponding image point must lie on the same circle. But there are infinitely many circles whose centers pass through the perpendicular bisector of a pre-image point and its corresponding image point. So the center must be where all the perpendicular bisectors of a pre-image point and its corresponding image intersect. Once that point is identified, the angle comes easily. Can you find a way of identifying first the angle and then the center?

The goal of this discussion is to point to the ways in which middle school work on transformations focuses mainly on visual apprehension and on identifying properties. However, since these properties are grasped visually, they are not always available for use in constructing images or symmetries.

Because students are familiar with these transformations when they enter high school, it is important to offer tasks for which visual apprehension will not suffice. It may also be necessary for students to identify and describe these properties as invariances across a range of examples. So, for example, in a dynamic geometry environment, students can become aware of the properties of reflection by observing how a shape and its image behave as they drag the shape or the line of reflection on the screen. Measurements of lengths and angles can help students turn these observations into more precise statements (for instance, "The line of reflection is the same distance from A as it is from A'"). Construction challenges, using either straightedge and compass or a DGE, can enable students to act on these observations: if the line of reflection is the same distance from A as it is from A', then to find the line of reflection, they need to find the midpoint of the segment AA'. Construction demands a discursive interaction, and this is why it is a crucial part of developing a geometric discourse.

In high school, the focus is on bringing other means of representation to work with transformations (such as coordinates, vectors, functions, and matrices). If students begin this work without having developed a language-based understanding of transformations, then they will be more and more challenged by tasks that are resolvable only through an application of definitions.

In middle school, transformations are largely seen as processes that turn one shape into another, as opposed to a function—a mathematical object. Repeated attention to shape A turning into shape B casts A as the initial object and B as the final one; there is a directionality—an arrow of time "before" and "after"—and even the language of pre-image and (after-)image reinforces this. Although perhaps surprising, this means that it can be difficult to think of B as an initial object.

This need to recognize reversibility is similar to the situation encountered in the elementary grades with regard to addition. Repeated exposure to statements such as $3 + 4 = \square$ ends up casting the right-hand side of the equation as the endpoint of the operation on the left. This makes it difficult for students to know how to handle statements such as $\square = 3 + 4$, or $3 + 4 = \square + 2$.

In the case of transformations, the difficulty that students often have in thinking of B as an initial object becomes evident when they are asked to work with compositions of transformations. Because B was the reflection of A, B can be hard for students to see now as the object to be reflected again into C—not to mention trying to forget B in order to relate A to C! In fact, when working on the composition of transformations, the focus is the transformation itself and not the shape being transformed. In other words, whereas middle school geometry draws attention to the process of turning A into B, high school geometry turns the process into an object ("reflecting" into "a reflection") and then *does things* with that object (in this case, composes it). This is a very important shift, which is often invisible, since students are quite able to use the words correctly (such as *reflecting* and *reflection*), without using them in the same way as the textbook or the teacher.

Teachers need to support this objectification process—namely, the process of turning a process into an object—in several ways for students to work successfully both with composition and with other representations of transformations. One way, which we have already mentioned, is to help students develop a more language-based understanding of the transformations through work with constructions. Another way is to change the roles of A and B (so that A is not always turning into B) by asking questions such as, "Now that you have reflected A to find B, what would happen if you reflected B, using the same line of reflection?" or, "B is the result of reflecting A across this line of reflection, but A was erased; can you recover it?"

For further discussion of transformations, see *Developing Essential Understanding of Geometry for Teaching Mathematics in Grades 6–8* (Sinclair, Pimm, and Skelin 2012).

Additional discussion of the equals sign appears in *Developing Essential Understanding of Equations, Expressions, and Functions for Teaching Mathematics in Grades 6–8* (Lloyd, Herbel-Eisenmann, and Star 2011).

Similarly, even before beginning work on composition, which focuses on transformations as objects, teachers might allow students to undertake a chain of transformations, such as reflecting *A* to obtain *B*, then rotating *B* to get *C*, and so on. Here, the focus would still be on the process of transforming, but the chain of transformations would provide instances of *B* also being an initial shape instead of always being just an ending shape.

One final way of supporting the process of objectification might involve having students work with the collection of symmetries of certain shapes. By determining whether—and by how much—a given shape can be rotated and superimposed on itself, for example, students shift their attention away from the process of rotating to the number of symmetries that the shape has. They will find that the square (see fig. 2.7a) rotates by 90, 180, 270, and, of course, 360 degrees, thus yielding rotational symmetry of order 4. They will discover that the rectangle appears to have rotational symmetry only of order 2 (see fig. 2.7b). Reflect 2.2 invites you to explore the rotational symmetries of other shapes.

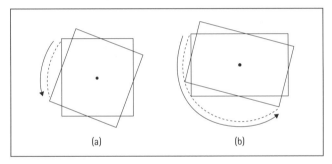

(a)   (b)

Fig. 2.7. Actions illustrating rotational symmetries of a square and a rectangle

Reflect 2.2

Explore the rotational symmetry of shapes other than the square and the rectangle. Can you find any shapes that have rotational symmetry of order 3? What about rotational symmetry of order 5?

We made an important choice here in working with the order of rotational symmetry—namely, that every shape has at least order 1 rotational symmetry, given that every shape overlaps itself after a rotation of 360 degrees. It would be natural to think a shape that has no rotational symmetry should have a rotational symmetry of order 0. But since it is convenient to define rotational symmetry of order n as rotations by an angle of $360°/n$ without changing the shape of the object, n cannot be allowed to be 0. This provides another small instance of where a definition is affected by a desire.

Yet more transformations: Linear algebra in postsecondary education

There are two main approaches to linear algebra: one is called "coordinate-free," and, we suppose, the other might be called "coordinate-full" (or "coordinate-expensive"). Students' first encounter with linear algebra is usually coordinate-full and full of matrix manipulations as well; a second encounter (usually in an abstract algebra course or possibly an honors linear algebra section) involves the study of vector spaces—and linear transformations of them—and matrices play a considerably smaller role.

Both types of linear algebra courses can be greatly enhanced by the use of geometry, especially in two and three dimensions. Earlier work in secondary school with transformations and isometries comes into play, providing both motivation and important imagery for what can otherwise, at times, degenerate into a mass of specific and uninformative calculations.

Shearing is a transformation that preserves area and parallelism, but not length, angle, or perpendicularity. See *Developing Essential Understanding of Geometry for Teaching Mathematics in Grades 6–8* (Sinclair, Pimm, and Skelin 2012).

Many intricate relations exist among the following related sets of ideas: isometries of the plane, 2×2 matrices, linear transformations of the plane, dilations, shears, and affine transformations of the plane. Unfortunately, in the short space we have here, we can only hint at some of the connections among these ideas and attempt to link them back to earlier points in this book and in *Developing Essential Understanding of Geometry for Teaching Mathematics in Grades 6–8* (Sinclair, Pimm, and Skelin 2012).

In what follows, think of a linear transformation as a transformation of the coordinate plane that preserves lines (i.e., collinearity relations) and, in particular, the origin. Examples of these transformations include rotating the plane around the origin, reflecting it across the line $y = x$, shearing parallel to the x- or y-axis, or dilating the plane with the center of dilation at the origin.

If we imagine the coordinate plane, a unit square has four key points that form the corners: (0, 0), (1, 0), (0, 1), and (1, 1). Under a general linear transformation, these points get mapped to (0, 0), (a, b), (c, d), and $(a + c, b + d)$. Notice that the origin always stays fixed, as every linear transformation maps the origin to itself. This means that neither non-identity translations nor glide reflections can be linear transformations, since they have no fixed points. The particular cases of rotations about the origin or reflections across a line that passes through the origin are linear transformations. Translations and glide reflections, rotations about a point that is not the origin, and reflections about a line that does not pass through the origin are all closely related to linear transformations and are examples of what are called *affine transformations*. An affine transformation is a linear transformation followed by a translation: in the case of a pure translation, the linear transformation involved is the identity transformation, which sends every point to itself. (As we mentioned in our discussion of Big Idea 4 in chapter 1, the identity transformation can be seen as a zero rotation or a zero translation, depending on definitions. But our preference is to see it as a zero rotation, not least because it is a linear transformation and has a simple matrix representation).

Notice that while in high school, transformations are typically categorized according to whether or not the transformation preserves size and shape; here, however, the categories of linear and affine transformations draw on very different properties. In other words, classification of isometries as linear or nonlinear transformations provides a different way to sort isometries from our usual categories of translations, reflections, rotations, and glide reflections. This alternative sorting is similar to, for example, sorting polygons into regular or non-regular ones instead of by means of our usual names for them (triangles, quadrilaterals, pentagons, and so on). It also makes one wonder whether there are other ways to categorize these transformations.

Under any linear transformation, the origin is always mapped to the origin, lines through the origin remain lines through the origin, and, in general, the unit square is transformed to a parallelogram (see fig. 2.8). We add "in general" to our claim to take care of some "monster" examples. Some linear transformations compress the whole plane onto a line through the origin, and, in one extreme case, the linear transformation whose matrix has all zero entries compresses the whole plane onto the origin itself.

A written proof is the endpoint of the process of proving.

Under linear transformations in three dimensions, the unit cube is transformed to a parallelopiped or compressed or collapsed onto a plane through the origin, onto a line through the origin, or onto the origin itself.

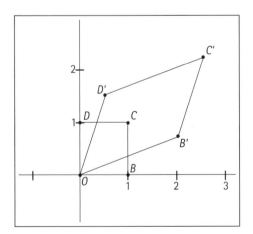

Fig. 2.8. Pre-image (unit square *OBCD*) and image (parallelogram *OB'C'D'*) under a linear transformation

Every linear transformation of the plane (equipped with the usual rectangular axes) can be associated with a 2 × 2 matrix, $\begin{pmatrix} a & b \\ c & d \end{pmatrix}$, and the diagram in figure 2.8 indicates that if we know where the points (1, 0) and (0, 1) get mapped, we know where *every* point in the plane goes—the entire transformation is determined just by knowing where these two particular points end up. When looking at a 2 × 2 matrix, the first column specifies where (1, 0) goes, and the second column specifies where (0, 1) goes.

Now, consider the following question: What is the area of the parallelogram that forms the image of the unit square? Instead of offering a detailed proof (part of which is an algebraic computation), we offer instead a diagram and a proof idea in figure 2.9. The figure shows the parallelogram (white) framed inside a rectangular area. Reflect 2.3 calls on you to provide reasons for claims implicit in the formulas about the shaded areas (and the shading itself reflects tacit claims about area equality of relevant triangles).

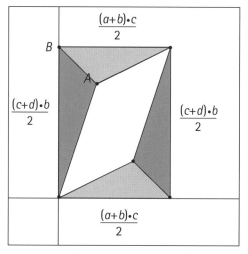

Fig. 2.9. Calculating the general parallelogram area

Reflect 2.3

Use the expressions in figure 2.9 to derive the area (white) of the parallelogram in the figure. What properties of parallelograms and triangles justify the intermediate calculations about triangle areas?

The numerical quantity for the white area, $(ad - bc)$, is known as the *determinant* of the matrix $\begin{pmatrix} a & b \\ c & d \end{pmatrix}$, and it may be positive or negative. If it is negative, then part of what the linear transformation does is a reflection about some line through the origin (which interchanges the order of the two axes and, in so doing, reverses orientation).

The absolute value of the determinant, $|ad - bc|$, gives the scale factor of magnification (or diminution) of area. All isometries that are also linear transformations (that is, certain reflections and rotations) have a scale factor of 1. In other words, they are area-preserving transformations. All such rotations have a determinant of +1 (preserving orientation), and all such reflections have a determinant of –1 (reversing orientation).

However, other linear transformations besides these can have a scale factor of 1 but are not isometries. For example, $\begin{pmatrix} 2 & 0 \\ 0 & 0.5 \end{pmatrix}$ has a scale of factor 1, so it is area preserving, although clearly it is not length preserving. The matrix represents a magnification (by a factor of 2) in the direction of the y-axis and a shrinking (by a factor of 0.5) in the direction of the x-axis. So while we might have hoped that we could define an isometry algebraically as an affine transformation whose linear transformation component had a scale factor of 1, this counterexample shows that such a definition is insufficient, in that it includes transformations that are not isometries. Some definition for *isometry* will be necessary to *prove* the classification theorem for isometries into four types (rotation, reflection, translation, and glide reflection).

In our discussion of coordinate geometry earlier in this chapter, we mentioned that some transformations were easily represented in terms of coordinates, such as reflection through the y-axis. Matrices make it easier to represent algebraically a much wider range of transformations. For example, the 2×2 matrix that effects a rotation counterclockwise about the origin through an angle of $\theta°$ to the positive x-axis is the following:

$$\begin{pmatrix} \cos(\theta) & -\sin(\theta) \\ \sin(\theta) & \cos(\theta) \end{pmatrix}$$

Figure 2.10 shows the unit square under such a rotation, and Reflect 2.4 asks you to explore the relationship between the matrix and the rotation.

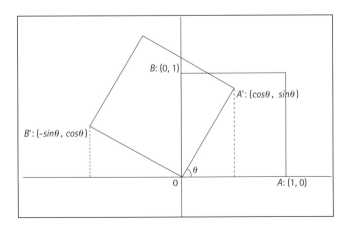

Fig. 2.10. Determining the coordinates of a rotated unit square

Reflect 2.4

How does the effect of the 2 × 2 matrix $\begin{pmatrix} \cos(\theta) & -\sin(\theta) \\ \sin(\theta) & \cos(\theta) \end{pmatrix}$, shown in figure 2.10, make sense, given what you now know about matrices and transformations?

As mentioned above, knowing where the two points (1, 0) and (0, 1) map to under a linear transformation determines the entire transformation, and the location of these two points are the column entries in the corresponding 2 × 2 matrix. Notice that its determinant is $\cos(\theta)^2 + \sin(\theta)^2 = +1$. To find the matrix of the identity transformation (seen as the zero rotation), set θ equal to 0. To find a clockwise rotation, substitute $-\theta$ for θ.

As our second example, the general matrix for a reflection about a line passing through the origin at an angle of $\theta°$ to the positive x-axis is the following:

$$\begin{pmatrix} \cos(2\theta) & \sin(2\theta) \\ \sin(2\theta) & -\cos(2\theta) \end{pmatrix}$$

Figure 2.11 shows a reflection of the unit square across a line of reflection that is at an angle of $\theta°$ to the positive x-axis. Notice that the trigonometric functions sine and cosine are closely implicated in the matrix specifications of both rotations and reflections in the plane.

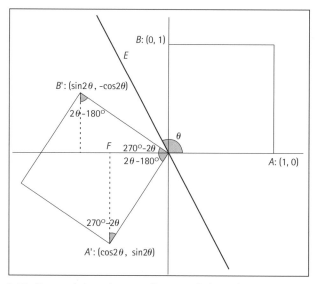

Fig. 2.11. Determining the coordinates of the reflected unit square

Much more, of course, can be said and studied about matrices and transformations and their properties. The following are just a few instances of assertions and related questions:

- Some dilations are linear transformations, as are some shears. Which ones? What are the specific forms of 2×2 matrices that carry out these types of transformations?

- Consider all the 2×2 matrices whose entries are 0 or 1. What is the geometric effect of the various different linear transformations specified by these matrices? (Edwina Michener (1978) calls these matrices the "basic sixteen.") What happens to the range of geometric transformations in the collection if you also allow –1 as an entry?

- Transformations that compress (or collapse) dimensions always have a scale factor of 0. Is the converse true?

- All linear transformations that do not compress (that have a non-zero determinant) have inverse linear transformations that undo their effect, giving rise to the inverse matrix. The inverse of
$\begin{pmatrix} a & b \\ c & d \end{pmatrix}$ is $1/(ad - bc) \begin{pmatrix} d & -b \\ -c & a \end{pmatrix}$. What is the determinant

of the inverse matrix? Can you see why? What does this say geometrically about scale factors? What does it say about whether you could have a reflection as an inverse to a rotation, or vice versa?

Our last point has to do with definition. Because students usually meet matrices before linear transformations (just as they meet transformations as processes in middle school before meeting them as objects—as types of a function—in high school), they come across matrix multiplication first, which is usually seen as both a complex and counterintuitive operation. Why is matrix multiplication defined the way it is?

The composition of two linear transformations will be another linear transformation, so the result of the composition will also have an associated matrix. The specific associated matrix relative to the two initial matrices (in order) is precisely that given by the (rather opaque) definition of matrix multiplication. For example,

$\begin{pmatrix} \cos(\theta) & -\sin(\theta) \\ \sin(\theta) & \cos(\theta) \end{pmatrix}$ represents a rotation of $\theta°$ counterclockwise

about the origin. Geometrically, the composition of this rotation with itself is another rotation, this one of $2\theta°$ counterclockwise about the origin. By the definition of matrix multiplication, this matrix product,

$$\begin{pmatrix} \cos(\theta) & -\sin(\theta) \\ \sin(\theta) & \cos(\theta) \end{pmatrix} \begin{pmatrix} \cos(\theta) & \sin(\theta) \\ \sin(\theta) & -\cos(\theta) \end{pmatrix}$$

is equal to

$$\begin{pmatrix} \cos^2(\theta) - \sin^2(\theta) & -2\cos(\theta)\sin(\theta) \\ 2\cos(\theta)\sin(\theta) & \cos^2(\theta) - \sin^2(\theta) \end{pmatrix}, \text{ or } \begin{pmatrix} \cos(2\theta) & -\sin(2\theta) \\ \sin(2\theta) & \cos(2\theta) \end{pmatrix},$$

which is clearly the matrix producing a rotation of $2\theta°$ counter-clockwise about the origin. Once again, an algebraic definition pre-cedes a geometric context that would allow it to make sense—not a desirable situation, especially in an educational setting.

Conclusion

Both of our cases of looking horizontally across the high school grades come from parts of the school geometry curriculum in which attention is often directed to numerical and algebraic tools and results. One goal of this chapter has been to show how the study of both coordinate geometry and trigonometry can begin with geometric thinking, including diagramming and constructing, and focusing on invariance. The geometric objects with which co-ordinate geometry and trigonometry concern themselves are worth constantly returning to since they provide the content on which it is possible to develop imagery and connections to facts and formulas.

In our vertical look at transformations, we have focused primarily on showing some of the complexity involved in the transition to grades 9–12 through the example of students' progress from thinking about transformations as processes to thinking about them as objects—a change that is crucial, not just for working with transformations, but also for thinking about functions more gen-erally. This complexity can be all the more difficult to appreciate when teachers and students are using the same words (e.g., *reflect* or *rotate*) but meaning very different things by them. Although we have simply pointed to the complexity in this chapter, our goals in the next chapter are to explore ways in which you can use the ideas developed in chapter 1 to offer your students strong support as they make the transition from grades 6–8 to grades 9–12 and prepare for postsecondary mathematics.

Chapter 3

Challenges: Learning, Teaching, and Assessing

Mathematics (particularly geometry) is shot through with infinity, to paraphrase the mathematics educator Caleb Gattegno (1984, p. 20; see also Beeney et al. 1982). Students need to appreciate that geometry is concerned with classes of problems, classes or families of configurations, and classes or families of properties. Theorems in geometry deal with invariance across a class or family. Teachers who see the study of geometry from this point of view can examine the textbook and other teaching materials (including geometry software) to select tasks that will repeatedly bring students up against variance and invariance.

There are no perfect lessons or tasks that you can find, adapt, or design that will help you enact the essential understandings and big ideas described in chapter 1. Instead, being aware of them might change the way in which you select and modify tasks for use in your classroom, as well as the ways in which you talk about the geometric objects, properties, and relationships under consideration. As a case in point, we present a lesson that is available on the NCTM Illuminations website for use at the high school level. We propose to examine it in the light of our big ideas and essential understandings. Our goal is not to evaluate the task; rather, it is to consider how familiarity with these big ideas might influence the way in which a teacher might work through the task in a classroom setting.

Case Study: "Perplexing Parallelograms"

The Illuminations lesson "Perplexing Parallelograms" enables students to explore congruence and similarity relationships among classes of parallelograms, to make and test conjectures, and to use deduction to establish the validity of these conjectures. The lesson begins with the activity sheet shown in figure 3.1.

Perplexing Parallelograms   NAME _____

For this investigation, complete the following steps:
- Choose one of the points along the diagonal of the parallelogram below, and label it point *P*.
- Through *P*, draw two line segments, one parallel to each pair of sides. As necessary, use a ruler, compass, or protractor.
- These two segments will divide the parallelogram into four smaller parallelograms. For reference, label the four smaller parallelograms *A*, *B*, *C*, and *D*.

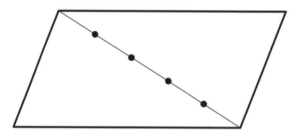

1. Measure the base and height of parallelograms *A*, *B*, *C*, and *D* to the nearest centimeter. Then, calculate the area of each parallelogram and record the results in the table below.

PARALLELOGRAM	AREA
A	
B	
C	
D	

2. What observations can you make regarding the areas of the four smaller parallelograms? What, if any, patterns emerge?

3. Compare your results with those of a classmate who chose a different point along the diagonal. Are your results similar? What results would you expect if you completed the same construction with a different parallelogram?

 ILLUMINΛTIONS   © 2008 National Council of Teachers of Mathematics
Resources for Teaching Math   http://illuminations.nctm.org

Fig. 3.1. "Perplexing Parallelograms" activity sheet

The Illuminations lesson "Perplexing Parallelograms is available at http://illuminations.nctm.org/LessonDetail.aspx?id=L709.

Students are first asked to choose one of the four points along the diagonal shown in the given parallelogram and to create four smaller parallelograms by drawing segments through their chosen point, *P*, parallel to the sides of the original parallelogram. They are then asked to measure areas of the resulting smaller parallelograms before making conjectures about their areas. Finally, the students are asked to compare their results with those of classmates who chose a different point *P*.

The configuration offered in this lesson provides an excellent starting point for a geometric investigation. Keeping in mind Big Idea 1, which emphasizes the centrality of working with diagrams, you might launch students' work in another way—you might hold back from offering the diagram on the activity sheet and instead ask students to draw or construct a few different parallelograms and also to draw in their diagonals. Then you could ask students to divide their parallelograms into four smaller parallelograms. Students might find this somewhat challenging, and, if so, you might ask them to simplify the problem by working with rectangles, which would provide a useful foreshadowing of the variations they could eventually create in order to make new conjectures, as discussed in Essential Understanding 2c. The students might have a range of diagrams by this point, with different ways of turning one parallelogram into four.

The students' work might involve a set of diagrams like those in figure 3.2, in which the parallelogram is first divided into four congruent parallelograms by using equally spaced lines parallel to a base, then equally spaced lines parallel to the other sides and, finally, non-equally spaced lines parallel to a side.

Big Idea 1

Working with diagrams is central to geometric thinking.

Essential
Understanding 2c

Examining the possible variations of an invariant situation can lead to new conjectures and theorems.

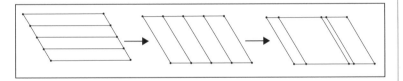

Fig. 3.2. Dividing a parallelogram into four parallelograms

By the time that students draw the third diagram, it may be clear that not much of interest is going on, since apart from the trivial case of congruent parallelograms, the variations produced by changing the spacing can produce an arbitrary set of parallelograms.

A second exploration might involve using one of the diagonals—for example, that shown as a dashed line in figure 3.3—and then its midpoint, to divide the parallelogram into four smaller, identical parallelograms. Varying the initial parallelogram might lead to the special case of the rectangle, shown in figure 3.3b. Choosing the other diagonal of the starting quadrilateral and its midpoint also results in four identical smaller parallelograms (see fig. 3.4a).

Moving from figure 3.4a to figure 3.4b involves varying the point along the diagonal where the vertices of the four smaller parallelograms meet. It results in a diagram in which the four parallelograms are obviously different from one another, and might even raise the questions, "Are they actually parallelograms?" and, "How would we know?"

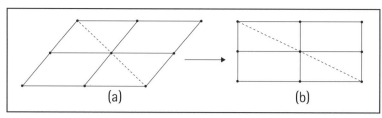

Fig. 3.3. Dividing the parallelogram into four congruent quadrilaterals

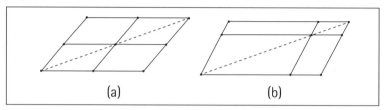

Fig. 3.4. Varying the point along the diagonal where the parallelograms meet

This last question strongly relates to Essential Understanding 3c. Grasping the shape visually differs from grasping the ideas about the shape suggested by a verbal definition—the latter requires some work to coordinate the definition of a parallelogram with the visual referent. The final variation shown in figure 3.4b leads to a whole family of sets of four quadrilaterals from the original starting one, for which the diagram in figure 3.4a is a special case—and the only instance in which the four parallelograms are the same size and shape.

It is not necessary to have all the students make all these diagrams. Before starting on the questions, you might ask the students to draw other variations of the diagram given on the activity sheet, so that they can attend to other questions about its particular properties and configurations (e.g., "Could its shape be different?" "Could the other diagonal be used?" "What is special about where the points have been placed?"). In addition to enabling students to interpret the diagram that has been presented more effectively, as we discussed in chapter 1 in connection with Essential Understanding 1c, the experience of creating diagrams enables geometric thinking and communicating, and thus helps pave the way for the eventual making and proving of conjectures, as we suggested in our discussion of Essential Understanding 1a. For example, just considering the fact that the diagram could have been created equally well by using the other diagonal will point to an additional invariance of the configuration.

The first question on the activity sheet in figure 3.1 directs students' attention to the areas of the four parallelograms without telling them what the conjecture should be. Although the students are asked to make observations and conjectures, this directing of their attention is likely to narrow the range of possibilities that they consider. If the students are to make conjectures, they need to identify an invariance—something that does not change while other things do. Indeed, Essential Understanding 2a asserts that invariance is at the heart of theorems and conjecture-making. Instead of focusing on the area, as question 1 does, another question might lead to the invariance perspective, by asking, "What happens to the configuration as you change the location of P?" This is essentially what question 3 is asking, but only after restricting the domain to the areas. Might there be some invariance in the perimeter? Or does changing P always produce similar parallelograms? It might even be worth noting that there is a strong symmetry in the changing of P, in that the variation as P moves from the midpoint to one vertex is identical to the variation of P as it moves from the midpoint to the other vertex.

Considering all the possible invariances will help draw attention to the fact that, as asserted in Essential Understanding 2b, invariances are rare—indeed, this is why it can be thrilling to find one. And before we move away from Big Idea 1, we should note that once the invariance related to areas of the parallelograms has been identified, the next geometric move is to find further variances, as Essential Understanding 2c suggests. For example, we might explore what happens to the theorem if the parallelogram turns into a rectangle, a square, or a rhombus. Or we might ask a similar question about a trapezoid or a kite.

The indirect goal of "Perplexing Parallelograms" is to work with the conjecture that the areas of two of the smaller parallelograms created in the activity are always equal, no matter what parallelogram or what point P students select. The applet "Parallelogram Exploration Tool" provided online with the lesson shows these parallelograms in the same color, as in figure 3.5. It is worth considering whether actually finding the areas is necessary. Indeed, in the applet (as well as in a DGE, which might be used alternatively), the areas are given (see fig. 3.6). Thus, when P is dragged along the diagonal, it is possible to see *both* varying and invariant properties: all the areas change, but the values of the two shaded ones are always the same.

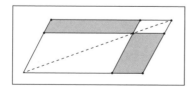

Fig. 3.5. Two (shaded) parallelograms with the same area

The dynamic geometry environment shows the invariance (and associated variance) in a more continuous and direct way than is possible with the paper-and-pencil version of the task. Observing

Essential ← **Understanding 2a**

Underlying any geometric theorem is an invariance— something that does not change while something else does.

Essential ← **Understanding 2b**

Invariances are rare and can only be appreciated when they emerge out of much greater variation.

Big Idea 1

Working with diagrams is central to geometric thinking.

Essential ← **Understanding 2c**

Examining the possible variations of an invariant situation can lead to new conjectures and theorems.

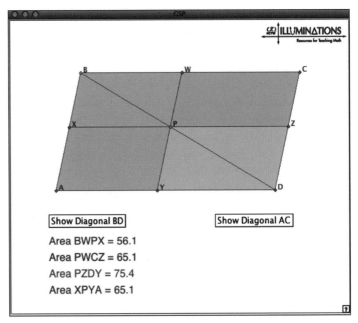

Fig. 3.6. The applet at the Illuminations site shows the areas of the parallelograms.

Muller (2010)
provides interesting
examples of
propositions of
claims developed
from explorations.
One type of task
that Muller suggests
is to use a DGE to
construct figures
based on textbook
theorems.

➡️ **Essential
Understanding 4c**

*Behind every proof is
a proof idea.*

the invariance in this way might well provoke surprise, which could support the move to explain how the two parallelograms in figure 3.5 can have the same area, even through they are not congruent. It is also the case that the two white parallelograms in the figure are similar, and a conjecture to that effect could be another fruitful one to pursue, though perhaps less interesting than the more surprising relationship between the two shaded parallelograms.

Why do these two parallelograms have the same area? Essential Understanding 4c underlines the importance of developing a proof idea. We might begin by thinking of the tools that we have for considering why the two areas are the same. We could focus on the formula for the area of a parallelogram—that is, the base times the height—and try to show that those products are the same for the two parallelograms. Or a second proof idea might be to relate the area of each parallelogram to other areas that we know something about—for example, we know that the diagonal line divides each of the white parallelograms in figure 3.5 into two congruent triangles. One way of drawing attention to this proof idea would be to ask students to consider the two shaded trapezoids in figure 3.7—trapezoids that seem to have particular properties worth investigating on their own right!

Still another strategy might be to use the principle of shearing. The parallelogram can be sheared into a rectangle without changing its area. This will also have the effect of turning both shaded parallelograms into rectangles. Now instead of trying to work with

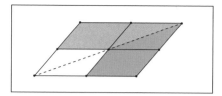

Fig. 3.7. Attending to the trapezoids in the diagram

See *Developing Essential Understanding of Geometry for Teaching Mathematics in Grades 6–8* (Sinclair, Pimm, and Skein 2012) for a discussion of how shearing, composition, and decomposition provide ways of both *seeing that* a measurement formula is the right one and *seeing why* it is the right one.

the areas of parallelograms (and thus, finding their heights), we only need to compare the areas of two rectangles. This could lead to a simplified version of the second proof idea—simplified in that the fact that a diagonal always cuts a rectangle into two congruent triangles might be more accessible than the corresponding result for a parallelogram.

Thinking about Assessment

The Illuminations lesson "Perplexing Parallelograms" suggests that the students prove another conjecture of their own as part of the assessment or that they prove a given conjecture (that the product of the areas of the two similar parallelograms is equal to the product of the areas of the two parallelograms that have the same area). The latter assessment task focuses on the production of a written proof, but the former includes more of the proving process—that is, the generation of a conjecture first. However, if we focus on Big Idea 1 and Big Idea 2, we might also want to design an assessment task that invites specific work with diagrams, as well as offering greater attention to the role of invariance in making the conjecture and proof.

So, for example, you might ask the students to complete the following sentence:

1. The conjecture that we made about the areas of the parallelograms asserts that as _____ changes, _____ stays the same.

In addition, again exploring the students' awareness of the importance of invariance, you might ask the following question:

2. Why was it difficult to make a conjecture about the perimeters of the four parallelograms?

Another form of assessment might involve shifting the initial assumption of the diagram and asking students to think about how this would affect the conjecture and the proof:

3. David made the following diagram [as shown in fig. 3.8], similar to the one you worked with, but with *P* anywhere

Big Idea 1

Working with diagrams is central to geometric thinking.

Big Idea 2

Geometry is about working with variance and invariance, despite appearing to be about theorems.

inside the parallelogram, not just on the diagonal. Are there still four parallelograms? Do the conjectures that you made before still hold? Find other ways of varying *P* so that you can make a new conjecture.

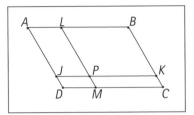

Fig. 3.8. Yet another way of creating four parallelograms from one

This task invites students to work with a given new diagram, to try to interpret it, and then to compare and contrast it with a more familiar one. It also invites the creation of new diagrams as students are asked to generate different ways of varying *P*. Finally, and most important, it enables students to work with the conjecture and proof *that they have already made* to see whether they understand the dependency relations involved.

Because the "Perplexing Parallelograms" task focuses mostly on conjecturing and proving, Big Idea 2 and Big Idea 4 are extremely salient. Also, we saw how an alternate approach to the task might elicit some of the essential understandings involved in Big Idea 1 in connection with diagramming. As we asserted, any talk about conjecturing and proving will necessarily involve variance and invariance, so that any task that calls on students to make conjectures or generate proofs can also be reinterpreted in terms of variance and invariance—and this is made even easier in the presence of DGEs.

In our discussion of this particular task, we did not mention Big Idea 3 at all, which addresses the role and status of definitions in geometry. Issues related to the definition of a parallelogram would certainly come up as students try to prove conjectures related to the diagram, such as that the two diagonals are always of the same length, that the opposite angles are always the same, or that the opposite sides are always the same length. Whether or not these statements need to be proved depends on which definition of the parallelogram is in use. They do if the definition of the parallelogram is that both pairs of opposite sides of the quadrilateral are parallel; but the defining property may be instead that the opposite angles are the same. Given that this task is about making conjectures and proofs related to congruence and similarity, it might be worth considering—with the students—which of these definitions would make their work easier (and why the definitions are equivalent, if indeed they are). After all, Essential Understanding 3*a* affirms that geometric objects can have different definitions and some may be better than others, depending on the context. Definitions

Big Idea 2

Geometry is about working with variance and invariance, despite appearing to be about theorems.

Big Idea 4

A written proof is the endpoint of the process of proving.

Big Idea 1

Working with diagrams is central to geometric thinking.

Big Idea 3

Working with and on definitions is central to geometry.

 Essential Understanding 3a

Geometric objects can have different definitions. Some are better than others, and their worth depends both on context and values.

are tools for geometric work, and if there is a choice, some might indeed be better suited to assisting with a particular geometric challenge than others.

The definition that gets used might well relate to the way that the students draw their initial diagrams or construct their parallelograms in a DGE. Another assessment task might involve starting with a parallelogram constructed according to one definition, and following its proof, starting again with a parallelogram constructed according to another. The two parallelograms shown in figure 3.9 look exactly the same, but their constructions are quite different. Might one be better than the other for the context of this task? Why?

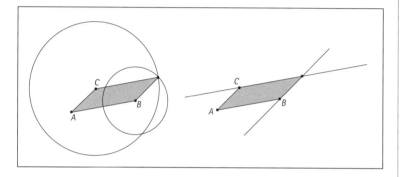

Fig. 3.9. Constructing a parallelogram

Because all geometric investigations involve known geometric objects, it is always possible to attend to the definitions that are in use and to ask whether others are possible or even better. Which definition would be the one to use when first verifying that the four shapes created in the diagram really are four parallelograms?

Conclusion

This book has developed four big ideas of geometry for teachers of mathematics in grades 9–12. The first one, focusing on the importance of diagrams in geometric thinking, emphasizes the way in which making diagrams can, in and of itself, develop awareness of the choices and constraints that are present in geometric objects but are not always evident in verbal statements or in one's geometric imagery. Indeed, we see one of the more important roles of diagramming as helping to develop richer visual imagery and, in particular, imagery to work with dynamically. This focus on dynamic imagery leads in Big Idea 2, which draws attention to the extent to which geometric properties, definitions, conjectures, and theorems can be seen as statements about invariances. To identify or make properties, definitions, conjectures, and theorems, one needs to be aware of the possible variability of a situation and, while pre-

Big Idea 1

Working with diagrams is central to geometric thinking.

Big Idea 2

Geometry is about working with variance and invariance, despite appearing to be about theorems.

Big Idea 3

Working with and on definitions is central to geometry.

Big Idea 4

A written proof is the endpoint of the process of proving.

serving that variability, home in on what is staying the same. By stating properties and definitions in terms of invariances, one is drawing attention to the various examples to which those properties and definitions apply. Definitions are the focus of Big Idea 3. We stressed the way in which definitions can and must change over time, as new conjectures are made, new examples are found, and new geometries are encountered. Rather than always being seen as the starting point of geometric work, definitions can also be the result of extensive investigation.

The three first big ideas provide the building blocks for Big Idea 4, the final big idea, which focuses on the process of proving. We exemplified the way in which the proving process involves working with diagrams, variation and invariance, conjectures, and definitions. We also drew attention to the important notion of argumentation, which can be used to identify the proof idea—which in turn can form the basis for a written, formal proof. Central to this big idea is the naming of certain strategies that can be used to make conjectures, such as the attention to symmetry and the use of what-if-not? thinking.

In chapter 2, we looked horizontally across the high school curriculum to show how the big ideas are relevant to working with coordinate geometry and trigonometry. We emphasized how these topics, which are usually approached in algebraic ways, can be understood in a more geometrical manner. Our vertical linking stretched down to transformations in the 6–8 grades and up to linear algebra at the postsecondary level.

The goal of chapter 3 was to show how the big ideas and essential understandings that we developed in chapter 1 might influence the way in which you think about or use tasks or lessons in the classroom. In particular, we focused on the way in which diagramming can be incorporated into a task, as well as the way in which the questions that you ask can draw attention to the varying and unvarying aspects of a given geometric configuration. We also showed possibilities for allowing room for the process of conjecturing—even when it seems that the conjecture has already been offered. Finally, we illustrated the kinds of proof ideas that can result from a geometric investigation and can aid in supporting a written proof. Our final section on assessment offered some alternative types of questions that you can pose on the basis of the four big ideas and, more important, how the essential understandings can shape the expectations that you have for your students' responses.

References

Balacheff, Nicolas. "Aspects of Proof in Pupils' Practice of School Mathematics." In *Mathematics, Teachers and Children: A Reader*, edited by David Pimm, pp. 216–35. London: Hodder and Stoughton, 1988.

Balacheff, Nicolas. "Is Argumentation an Obstacle? Invitation to a Debate." *Preuve: International Newsletter on the Teaching and Learning of Mathematical Proof* (May-June 1999). http://www-didactique.imag.fr/preuve/Newsletter/990506Theme/990506ThemeUK.html.

Barnett-Clarke, Carne, William Fisher, Rick Marks, and Sharon Ross. *Developing Essential Understanding of Rational Numbers for Teaching Mathematics in Grades 3–5*. Essential Understanding Series. Reston, Va.: National Council of Teachers of Mathematics, 2010.

Bartolini Bussi, Maria, and Mara Boni. "Instruments for Semiotic Mediation in Primary School Classrooms." *For the Learning of Mathematics* 23 (June 2003): 15–22.

Beeney, Roger, Mike Jarvis, Dick Tahta, John Warwick, and Derek White. *Geometric Images*. Derby, UK: Association of Teachers of Mathematics, 1982.

Brown, Stephen I., and Marion I. Walter. *The Art of Problem Posing*. 2nd ed. Hillsdale, N.J.: Lawrence Erlbaum Associates, 1990.

Cooney, Thomas J., Sybilla Beckmann, and Gwendolyn M. Lloyd. *Developing Essential Understanding of Functions for Teaching Mathematics in Grades 9–12*. Essential Understanding Series. Reston, Va.: National Council of Teachers of Mathematics, 2010.

Coxeter, Harold S. M. *Projective Geometry*. New York: Springer, 1987.

Dougherty, Barbara J., Alfinio Flores, Everett Louis, and Catherine Sophian. *Developing Essential Understanding of Number and Numeration for Teaching Mathematics in Prekindergarten–Grade 2*. Essential Understanding Series. Reston, Va.: National Council of Teachers of Mathematics, 2010.

Eisenstein, Elizabeth L. *The Printing Revolution in Early Modern Europe*. Cambridge: Cambridge University Press, 1983.

Ellis, Amy B., Kristen Bieda, and Eric Knuth. *Developing Essential Understanding of Proof and Proving for Teaching Mathematics in Grades 9–12*. Essential Understanding Series. Reston, Va.: National Council of Teachers of Mathematics, forthcoming.

Fauvel, John. "Unit 4: The Greek Study of Curves." *Topics in the History of Mathematics*. Milton Keynes, UK: The Open University, 1987.

Fauvel, John, and Jeremy Gray, eds. *The History of Mathematics: A Reader.* Basingstoke, UK: Macmillan Education, 1987.

Fourier, Joseph, and Gaspard Monge. "Une Discussion sur la Ligne Droite." *Mathesis* 9 (1883): 139–41. Reprinted from "Géométrie Descriptive" (Monge, Professeur), *Séances de l'Ecole Normale, Débats*, vol. 1, pp. 28–33 (February 14, 1795).

Frege, Gottlob. *The Foundations of Arithmetic: A Logico-Mathematical Enquiry* (1884). 2nd rev. ed. New York: Harper and Brothers, 1960.

Gattegno, Caleb. "Infinity." *Mathematics Teaching* 107 (June 1984): 19–21.

Healy, Lulu, Reinhard Hoelzl, Celia Hoyles, and Richard Noss. "Messing Up." *Micromath* 10 (Spring 1994): 14–16.

Henderson, David, and Daina Taimina. *Experiencing Geometry: Euclidean and Non-Euclidean with History.* Upper Saddle River, N.J.: Prentice-Hall, 2006.

Hollebrands, Karen, Colette Laborde, and Rudolf Sträßer. "Technology and the Learning of Geometry at the Secondary Level." In *Research on Technology and the Teaching and Learning of Mathematics*, vol. 1, edited by M. Kathleen Heid and Glendon Blume, pp. 155–205. Charlotte, N.C.: Information Age Publishing, 2008.

Lakatos, Imre. *Proofs and Refutations: The Logic of Mathematical Discovery*, Cambridge: Cambridge University Press, 1976.

Lannin, John, Amy B. Ellis, and Rebekah Elliott. *Developing Essential Understanding of Mathematical Reasoning for Teaching Mathematics in Prekindergarten–Grade 8*. Essential Understanding Series. Reston, Va.: National Council of Teachers of Mathematics, 2011.

Leung, Allen. "Dragging in a Dynamic Geometry Environment through the Lens of Variation." *International Journal of Computers in Mathematics Learning* 13 (July 2008): 135–57.

Lloyd, Gwendolyn, Beth Herbel-Eisenmann, and Jon Star. *Developing Essential Understanding of Expressions, Equations, and Functions for Teaching Mathematics in Grades 6–8*. Essential Understanding Series. Reston, Va.: National Council of Teachers of Mathematics, 2011.

Manin, Yuri I. *A Course in Mathematical Logic*. New York: Springer, 1977.

Michener, Edwina Rissland. "Understanding Understanding Mathematics." *Cognitive Science* 2 (October/December 1978): 361–83.

Molland, George. "Shifting the Foundations: Descartes' Transformation of Ancient Geometry." *Historia Mathematica* 3 (February 1976): 21–49.

Muller, Kimberly. "How Technology Can Promote the Learning of Proof." *Mathematics Teacher* 103 (February 2010): 437–41.

National Council of Teachers of Mathematics (NCTM). *Principles and Standards for School Mathematics.* Reston, Va.: NCTM, 2000.

———. *Curriculum Focal Points for Prekindergarten through Grade 8 Mathematics: A Quest for Coherence.* Reston, Va.: NCTM, 2006.

———. *Focus in High School Mathematics: Reasoning and Sense Making.* Reston, Va.: NCTM, 2009.

Netz, Reviel. "Greek Mathematical Diagrams: Their Use and Their Meaning." *For the Learning of Mathematics* 18 (November 1998): 33–39.

Pólya, George. *Mathematics and Plausible Reasoning.* Vol. 1, *Induction and Analogy in Mathematics.* Princeton, N.J.: Princeton University Press, 1954/1990.

Sinclair, Nathalie, David Pimm, and Melanie Skelin. *Developing Essential Understanding of Geometry for Teaching Mathematics in Grades 6–8.* Essential Understanding Series. Reston, Va.: National Council of Teachers of Mathematics, 2012.

Thom, René. "'Modern' Mathematics: An Educational and Philosophic Error?" *American Scientist* 59 (November/December 1971): 695–99.

Zbiek, Rose Mary. "The Pentagon Problem: Geometric Reasoning with Technology." *Mathematics Teacher* 89 (February 1996): 86–90.

Titles in the Essential Understanding Series

The Essential Understanding Series gives teachers the deep understanding that they need to teach challenging topics in mathematics. Students encounter such topics across the pre-K–grade 12 curriculum, and teachers who understand the related big ideas can give maximum support as students develop their own understanding and make vital connections.

Developing Essential Understanding of—

Forthcoming:

Developing Essential Understanding of—

Visit www.nctm.org/catalog for details and ordering information.